Put Your Hands into Hers

Mary,
Our Life, Our Sweetness,
and
Our Hope ...

REV. RONALD RAMSON, C.M.

Archway Publishing books may be ordered through booksellers or by contacting:

Archway Publishing
1663 Liberty Drive
Bloomington, IN 47403
www.archwaypublishing.com
844-669-3957

ISBN: 978-1-6657-0513-4 (sc)
ISBN: 978-1-6657-0515-8 (hc)
ISBN: 978-1-6657-0514-1 (e)

Library of Congress Control Number: 2021906423

Print information available on the last page.

Archway Publishing rev. date: 07/01/2021

Contents

Note

Opposite the western side of our residence here in Perryville, Missouri is what many call "The Bronze Mary."

People—locals, and tourists—kneel before her at the prie-dieu and put their hands into her hands. Many times, I have done the same.

The Association of The Miraculous Medal, in the middle of the Fall of the past year, asked me to place into Mary's hands, several thousand prayer requests. I placed one stack after the other into her hands and then blessed each one. What a great privilege! Have you got prayer intentions?

Are you looking for hope, for inspiration, for compassion?

Put your hands into hers.

****

This is not a textbook on Mariology or a theological treatise. It is a book on and about Mary from a Vincentian priest who has had Mother Mary in his mind and heart for over seventy-five years. You will read autobiographical snippets of me throughout the book.

Preface/Background

I am surrounded by Mary. I am referring to Mary, the Mother of Jesus.

The Church of the Assumption, now referred to as the Shrine Church (it houses the National Shrine of Our Lady of the Miraculous Medal), stands in dominance to the left side fairly near the residence in which I live. Close to the church is a small center housing a religious goods store and a meeting room named after Saint Catherine Laboure.

To the west, alongside us, runs the Rosary Walk leading to three grottoes.

Farther west and parallel to our residence lies the office building of the Association of the Miraculous Medal in which women and men dedicated to the ministry of Mary work.

Behind us, "in our back yard," is the Marian Meditation Walk. I prefer to call it the "Ring of Mary" or the "Crown of Mary" because within the circle stand twelve statues of Mary with one immediately off to the side.

These thirteen statues represent Mary's unflinching love for humankind. Each statue shows Mary in a different physical appearance, in native dress, related to the time and culture. She is a master of appropriateness. I always have been amazed how young girls have been able to describe in detail the dress of Mary and her shoes (if she was wearing any). And Mary is a master of languages and dialects!

These thirteen Marys cover the globe: Portugal, England, Ireland, France, Germany, Poland, Italy, Mexico, Japan.

I have been blessed over the last two years by making fifty-plus videos for the Association of the Miraculous Medal. The videos were all made either at "The Bronze Mary" or at "The Marian Meditation Walk" or at one of the Marian grottos.

What does Mary have to say to you and me today? We have gone through an epic pandemic with world changing aftereffects. A small virus has changed the world like, perhaps, nothing else could with such rapidity and expansiveness.

Is Mary a valid intercessor for today or a relic of the past, nice to know of, nice to look at, but nothing more?

What do many pray? "Hail, holy Queen, our life, our sweetness, and out hope."

Does Mary inspire our hearts and minds?

Is she a vessel of hope?

Do we feel a mother's love?

A Few Basic Remarks

A Few Basic Remarks

Why?

Why write another book about Mary who lived two-thousands years ago? There are so many publications on her available. I personally have a dozen Marian books on my shelf.

Maybe the reason—why—is because there are a good number of people out in the pews or at home who think alike: Mary is the answer to a messed up world. Mary is our refuge and our hope.

I was asked to write this book on Mary by a reputable editor, so I have. I had no intention to author a book on Mary; it never entered my mind, but I believe in divine providence. I believe that God speaks to us through persons, circumstances, situations. I have had good examples of this in my life. When that editor asked me to write a book on Mary, I saw this as God's will. And guess what? Almost immediately, I became flooded with Marian ideas, including the title for the book!

Your purchase of this book is an example of God speaking to you and Mary doing her part also. Am I pushing the envelope or is there truth to my assumption?

The writing of this book has been a daunting task yet one of joy. As I have been in lockdown for months, I utilized the time for prayer, research, and writing.

As we have lived through the pandemic, we often have invoked Our Lady Health of the Sick (her feast day is the Saturday before the last Sunday in August). I filmed a short video on Mary under this title for the Association of the Miraculous Medal and was amazed at the number of peoples' responses! Obviously, people see the need for Our Lady during this turbulent time.

Added to the fire of the pandemic has been the unrest and turmoil on our city streets. This is reminiscent of the July 1830 uprisings in Paris as foretold by Mary to Saint Catherine Laboure.

We need Mary; we need a mother's love in action. We need her bonafide inspiration. We need her truth, compassion, justice. Mary can and will give all five! You will read those words over and over within these pages.

Consequently, this book: **"Put Your Hands into Hers."**

Three Essentials

Three essential concepts intentionally run through this book, if not explicitly certainly implicitly: a mother's love, hope, and inspiration.

In all the apparitions of the Mother of Jesus to persons throughout the centuries, she has exemplified three qualities: a mother's love, hope, and inspiration. Yes, at times, she has given people a mission, but underlying that mission are those salient qualities.

A Mother's love.

We only can speculate, but there must have been a conversation between Jesus and his mother that ran something like this:

> "Mother, after all these years here at Nazareth earning
> a living as a carpenter and caring for you after dear
> father Joseph's death, the time has come. I will be
> leaving for Jerusalem where I will be initiating my
> mission: preaching the Kingdom of God. I have talked
> to our family members and neighbors to keep their

eye on you. Our savings are in my cabinet drawer; you should not have any financial problems. I will see you occasionally, certainly at the wedding in Cana."

Her husband, Joseph had passed; now the love of her life, Jesus, was leaving her. She had to know within her that he would suffer in many ways during his public ministry.

Her mother's love was strained when he was twelve years old, when Joseph and she found him in the temple of Jerusalem. She had been worried to death for three days.

Now as a grown adult she will have more to worry about than a lost pre-teen. She knew what Jesus has to say will clash with religious authorities and no doubt with the Roman occupational forces. A mother's love is without borders.

In every apparition, Mary our Mother, has manifested a Mother's love regardless of age, country, recipient.

A mother's love is:

> nondefinable,
> the most powerful force in the world,
> unconditional and eternal,
> sacrificial,
> beyond generosity,
> the total gift of self.

Hope.

While missioned in Denver, I saw the musical "Damn Yankees" starring Jerry Lewis; I thoroughly enjoyed the stage production. One of the hit songs is "Heart."

> "You've gotta have hope
> Mustn't sit around and mope

Nothin's half as bad as it may appear." [1]

Moving from the profane to the spiritual, Saint Paul tells us:

"Now hope that is seen is not hope.
For who hopes for what he sees?
But if we hope for what we do not see,
we wait for it with patience."[2]

A husband and father, a Frenchman, a man beatified by the Church said:

"Hope! The fault of many Christians is to hope
little....
They are apostles in the boat during the storm: they
forget that the Savior is in the midst of them."[3]

The year of 2020 was a tough one. Those of us who faced the consequences of the coronavirus, needed to rely on hope. We waited and waited in lockdown praying and hoping against hope. We looked for the vaccine; it was our hope for freedom.

It would be great ingratitude towards Divine Providence not to hope.[4]

The only language Mary speaks is hope for the present or future. She is our anchor.

Hope is a life-long task; we hold on to it with both hands often like in a roller-coaster. Hope is a fuel that keeps us burning.

Saint Padre Pio tells us:

---

[1] Damn Yankees, lyrics by Richard Adler and Larry Ross. Damn Yankees(/d/ damnyankees.htm

[2] + Romans 8:24-25

[3] Letter #599, Antoine-Frederic Ozanam to Dominic Meynis, January 29, 1845, Paris

[4] Letter # 1171, Antoine-Frederic Ozanam to Abbe Henri Maret, September 14, 1852, from Biarritz, France

"Pray, hope, and don't worry."

I believe that he is right, but...

I am afraid that we do not pray enough or hope enough, and we worry too much. Am I wrong?

Saint Augustine tells us:

"The deeper our faith, the stronger our hope."[5]

"Hope is being able to see that there is light despite all of the darkness." (Desmond Tutu)

Inspiration

Inscription is something that makes us want to do something or that gives us the idea to do or create. Inspiration: a force or influence that inspires us. Inspiration can be a person, experience, a word that makes us want to do or create or compose, etc.

We see this in the person of the Mother of God in all her apparitions; she inspires persons, whatever their age. She inspires you and me today by thoughts of her running in our minds and in our hearts.

"Marian spirituality is finding the inspiration to follow Christ in Mary."[6]

---

[5] From a letter to Proba, Liturgy of the Hours, Vol. IV, p. 408
[6] Marian Spirituality and the Vincentian Charism, Corpus Delgado, C.M., Vincentiana, Vol. 46, #4, p.1

A Marian Inspirational Gallery

"Don't Be Afraid"

I think that the most frequent command in all Sacred Scripture is:

"Don't be afraid."

We read the phrase in the Bible 365 times.

Moses was attracted to the burning bush. And, as he drew near, he heard the voice of God:

> "Come no nearer! Remove the sandals from your feet,
> for the place where you stand is holy ground....Moses
> hid his face, for he was afraid to look at God."[7]

What do we read in the Letter to the Hebrews?
"Our God is a consuming fire."[8]
What do we read earlier in the Letter to the Hebrews?
"It is a fearful thing to fall into the hands of the living God."[9]
In the seventy-two books of Sacred Scripture we read that to be in the presence of God is a fearful thing. When God enters a person's life in a dramatic fashion as in the case of Moses and others, people are afraid and rightly so. Wherever God comes and manifests his presence, it is holy ground; people take off their sandals.

To be in the presence of God, either directly or indirectly through

---

[7] Exodus 3: 2, 5, 6
[8] Hebrews 12:29
[9] Ibid., 10:31

his messengers, the angels (that is what the word "angel" means), e.g., the Archangels Michael, Gabriel, Raphael, it is a fearful thing as the Letter to the Hebrews tells us.

In reviewing the Book of the New Testament, primarily in the four gospels, as the life and actions of our Lord and Savior enfold, we sense a lessening of being afraid of God and drawing closer to him. The fact is that he wants us to be in an intimate relationship with him. Jesus tells us: "I am the Good Shepherd," "I am the vine, you are the branches."

We remember the disciples of Jesus going up to Jerusalem with him:

> "...they were amazed, and those who followed were afraid."[10]

Consider the Transfiguration. Jesus took Peter, James, and John up the mountain to prayer.[11] And they see Jesus' glory and Moses and Elijah appear from the dead after centuries. And from a cloud came a voice that said,

> "This is my beloved Son, with whom I am well pleased; listen to him."

> "When the disciples heard this, they fell prostrate and were very much afraid but Jesus came and touched them, saying, 'Rise and do not be afraid."[12]

It is a fearful thing to fall into the hands of the living God.

What do we hear in spirituality? We are called to have "a reverential fear" of God.

What does that mean? The etymology of "reverence" means "to

---

[10] Mark 10:32
[11] Matthew 17:1
[12] Matthew 17: 6

stand in awe of, of fear." We respect our creator, our sustainer, our redeemer, our love. We respect God's power and authority; we want to please him. God is our Father, our Parent.

A passage from Hebrews that I have found more than interesting is:

> "In the days of his flesh, Jesus offered up prayers and supplications, with loud cries and tears. And he was heard for his godly fear."[13]

Do we offer up prayers with loud cries and tears? Are we heard for our reverential fear?

The Archangel Gabriel tells Mary:

> "Do not be afraid, Mary, for you have found favor with God."[14]

After her Assumption into heaven, Mary appears throughout the centuries to people, very often, but not exclusively, to youngsters and teenagers. Yes, she does appear to adults but, in my judgement, to those men and women who probably manifest child-like qualities in their demeanor or people who possess strong faith.

What is it about children and Mary? In general, they are more innocent, more at ease, more observant, more curious. They do not have the hang ups of adults. They do possess sinful habits like adults.

In my research of many Marian apparitions, I have not read Our Lady saying to children or adults: "Don't be afraid." Why not? Because Mary's physical beauty overwhelms people, and she progressively gets more beautiful in prolonged apparitions. Her clothes are appealing, colorful, and decorative. Children can describe Mary's dress in ultimate detail.

Whenever she wears a crown, it is so impressive, often with twelve

---

[13] Hebrews 5:7 In one translation, it reads that he was heard "because of his reverence."
[14] Luke 1:30

stars. She smiles; she sings along, she keeps time with the music. Is this not attractive?

We are dealing with a Mother, but not an ordinary mother or even an extraordinary mother. We are talking about the Mother of God, the spiritual Mother of humankind gifted to us by Jesus himself not at the Last Supper but at the last breaths of his earthy life.

Mother Mary tells people to "Come, come to me" or words of that effect. She touches people's hearts. In a few cases, she physically touches visionaries. Her appearances have calming effects; they have a serenity about them. Often, Our Lady has the Child Jesus with her. What is more loving than a baby? Who would not want to hold the baby Jesus?

What do we expect from any mother? Mary is our heavenly Mother, our spiritual Mother. She is our living Mother who is with us our whole lives. She never leaves us for any reason. She wants our love and affection as much as we want hers! Is it not wonderful?!

Mary's Biography by Saint Maximus the Confessor[15]

About eleven years ago, I gave a day of prayer to the diocesan collegian seminarians at Holy Trinity Seminary, Irving, Texas, in the Diocese of Dallas. I based one of my presentations on the life of the Blessed Mother, and I used the thoughts of Saint Maximus the Confessor's biography of Mary. It is unique. It is far different from the gospel accounts.

I want to share with you some of Saint Maximus' major thoughts for your prayerful reflection.

In Saint Maximus biography, we see that Mary is a lifelong companion in Jesus's mission, a leader of the early church that we read about in the Acts of the Apostles.

She is the source of many gospel stories about Jesus' life. Saint Luke must have had Mary's input for the first part of his gospel; how else, for example, could he had known those infancy accounts?

Maximus portrays Our Lady as a lifelong companion in her Son's mission, and, as I said, a source of a good number of gospel scenarios about Jesus' ministry.

The saint has constructed his material from canonical biblical sources and known apocryphal material as well as sources unknown

---

[15] St. Maximus the Confessor—580-662 I recommend an article in Commonweal, "Maximus's Mary" of November 30, 2009. I personally did not use this article here; I used another source.

to us today, especially those related to the Passion and to Our Lady's Assumption (or Dormition).

Maximus' "Life of the Virgin" assumes that other women played significant roles in the early church besides Our Lady.

One of the things most unusual in the biography is not only Mary's close companionship with her Son Jesus but the leading role she and other women took in his mission. Mary constantly stands beside him, always understanding his teachings. Maximus tells us that many women followed Jesus as disciples, and the Mother of the Lord guided and advised these women, acting as their mediator with her Son.

Perhaps most striking in the biography is Mary's central presence throughout her Son's Passion. This begins with that night of the Last Supper. She is the source of most of the information in the gospels about her Son that day, the only person who stayed with him from his arrest to the Resurrection. She saw and heard everything. When she was prevented from Jesus' appearances before Annas and Caiphas, she got information from eyewitnesses.

The Mary in Saint Maximus' life is a deeply grieving mother during her Son's final trials. She overcomes her fear of crowds (I presume they were somewhat hostile) and armed soldiers who accompany Jesus on his "via crucis." She stands beneath the cross to the bitter end with Saint John.

Maximus says that most of the words and actions before Jesus' death were recounted to the apostles and other disciples by the Blessed Mother herself. Later, Mary becomes a teacher to the apostles, the one to whom they report, the one who maintains the unity, order, and doctrine of the early church.

Who are we to question Maximus' biography?

Is it 100% accurate? I personally do not know, but I have liked what I have read over the years.

Mary, The New Eve[16]

I remember years ago in scripture class during study on the Book of Genesis; we learned of the "first gospel" or, as it is called, "The Protoevangelium."

God revealed the battle between the Woman and the serpent, and his defeat at the hands of her Son:

> "The Lord God said to the serpent…I will put enmity between you and the woman, and between your seed and her seed; he shall bruise your head, and you shall bruise his heel."[17]

We always referred to these verses as the "First Good News."

I look at the front of Miraculous Medal and what do I see? The Blessed Virgin Mary with her foot crushing the head of the serpent, the devil!

We must remember something: The Blessed Virgin herself designed this medal. Mary portrays herself crushing the head of the serpent. She is the bearer of the First Good New.

By reflecting on the writings of Saint Paul, e.g., in Galileans 4:4, I Corinthians 15:21-22, Romans 5:19), and other scriptures, the early Church began to see Mary as the image of the 'new Eve."

Saint Irenaeus around 180 AD says:

---

16 I recommend Scott Hahn's The Lamb's Supper, Doubleday, 1999, p. 79-80
17 Genesis 3:14-15

"Just as Eve…..having become disobedient, was made the cause of death for herself and for the whole human race, so also Mary…being obedient, was made the cause of salvation for the whole human race…."

Saint Jerome reminds us:

"Death through Eve, life through Mary."

These two quotes alone illustrate the importance of Our Lady's role in Christ's redemption.

Eve was called "mother of the living, and Mary "the Mother of living in the order of grace." What depth is here!

Our Blessed Virgin Mary's role as the "new Eve" expresses not only her relationship to her Son Jesus but also to us children of God and heirs to heaven.

Her role in our salvation is not primary as that of Jesus, nonetheless, it is part of God's plan. Remember, at the Annunciation, Mary said "yes" to Gabriel, and our salvation began.

You and I acknowledge Our Lady's role in salvation as the "new Eve." We refer to the hill on Calvary when Jesus gifted us with his Mother. She truly is "the second Eve."[18]

"Truly, you are blessed among women.
For you have changed Eve's curse
into a blessing, and Adam, who hitherto
lay under a curse, has been blessed
because of you."[19]

---

[18] I attempted to simplify some more complexed Mariology. If you have a copy of The Catechism of the Catholic Church you will find helpful materials in numbers # 411, 494, 504-505. There is a great beauty in mediating on Mary the New Eve! I recommend praying to Mary the New Eve which is an ancient title of Our Lady.

[19] Sermon by Saint Sophronius, Breviary, Vol. 1, p. 1622

Saint Elizabeth Ann Seton and Mary in Italy

Elizabeth Ann Seton, her husband William, and their oldest daughter Anna Maria sailed from New York to Livorno, Italy on October 2, 1803. They traveled with the hope that the warmer climate of Italy would improve William's health.

Unfortunately, William died on December 27. 1803. After burial, Elizabeth and Anna Maria, Anglicans, moved in with their friends the Filicchis, devout Roman Catholics.

One day, Elizabeth Ann noticed a little prayer of Mrs. Filicchi on the table. It was the prayer of Saint Bernard of Clairvaux to the Blessed Virgin. Elizabeth Ann was moved:

> "…Begging her to be our Mother, and I said to her, with the certainty that God would surely refuse nothing to his Mother, and that she could not help living and pitying the poor souls he died for, that I felt really I had a Mother…"[20]

I must believe that the prayer that Elizabeth Ann was referring to had to be "The Memorare". The prayer has been attributed to Saint Bernard.[21] In the prayer, the saint calls upon Mary as "my Mother,"

---

[20] Mrs. Seton, Joseph I. Dirvin, C.M., Farrar, Straus and Company, New York, 1962, p.138
[21] Saint Bernard 1090-1153

and "O Mother of the Word Incarnate" "in your mercy hear and answer" his petitions.

The Filicchis took the two Setons on a trip to Florence. In the Church of Santa Maria Novella, Elizabeth Ann was again deeply moved.

> "A picture of the Descent from the Cross...engaged my whole soul – Mary at the foot of it expressed well that the iron had entered into hers, and the shades of death over her agonized countenance so strongly contrasted the heavenly peace of the dear Redeemer that it seems as if his pains had fallen on her. How hard it was to leave that picture, and how often, even in the few hours' interval since I have seen it, I shut my eyes and recall it in imagination!"[22]

The Filicchis made a pilgrimage to the shrine of La Madonna del Grazie on Montenero, the most famous in Tuscany. The two Setons attended Mass in the church. Above the altar was the gem-encrusted Virgin.

Elizabeth wrote:

> "I am a mother, so the mother's thought came also. How was my God a little babe in the first stage of his mortal existence in Mary? But I feel these thoughts in my babes at home, which I daily long for more and more."[23]

I do not claim that I am an expert in the life of Elizabeth Ann Seton. I am not, but from my studies of her, I am convinced that she was born to be a mother; that was her vocation in life. She was a

[22] Mrs. Seton, pp. 133-134
[23] Ibid., p. 136

mother to her children; she was a mother to her religious sisters that she birthed. Elizabeth Ann saw Our Lady as the Mother of Jesus, the Mother who nestled Jesus in her arms as a baby, who held him in her arms after he was taken down from the cross. Mary is our Mother today because her Son gave her to us. In every apparition of Mary, she comes to us as a Mother. Her words or her silence or her presence is that of a mother.

On every occasion Mary is our life, our sweetness, and our hope.

"After God...."

Every time I pull up a book of the life of Saint Jean-Marie Vianney, I read his words:

> "After God, I owe all to my mother.
> She was so good! Virtue passes readily from the heart
> of a mother into that of her children."[24]

How many can repeat those words of The Cure of Ars? His mother must have been quite a woman!

His father, Matthieu, and mother, Marie, were parents of six children; Jean-Marie was the fourth. If he could say such flattering words about his mother as the fourth child, what would the other five say?

Can we say: "After God, I owe all to my mother? She was so good!" Is this statement too braggadocios, too bold? Or too unfitting?

Could we say at this moment of our lives?

> "After God, I owe a lot to Mother Mary.
> She has helped me through quite a bit in my
> relationship with God?"

Mary has certainly been an inspiration and a Mother in my life, also an anchor of hope during the storms of life.

What about you?

---

[24] "The Cure of Ars: Saint Jean-Marie Baptiste Vianney," Abbe Francis Trochu, Newman Press, Westminister, MD, 1950, p.10

Mary's Mom and Dad: Jesus' Grandparents

Traditionally in our Church, we celebrate the parents of the Blessed Virgin Mary on July 26: The Feast of Saints Anne and Joachim.

Most of the information that we possess on them comes from an apocryphal writing known as the Protoevangelium of James the Lesser, author unknown (elsewhere in this book I have mentioned this work).

The writing is dated about 150 A.D. In the beginning of the Protoevangelium, Joachim and Anne in their old age are both lamenting the fact that they have had no children. An angel appears to Anne and promises her that she will conceive. Anne shares this apparition with Joachim, and both are ecstatic. They manifest a deep confidence in God, and a child is born, a girl whom they name Miriam (Mary).

The couple dedicate their daughter to God, keeping her from sin and evil. At three years old, they entrusted Mary in the temple where pious women brought up young girls consecrated to the Lord.

The man Joseph is named her protector when she reaches twelve or thirteen years of age. He is selected by God as her betrothed.

A few thoughts:

+ Joachim was of the royal house of David.
  Anne was of Levitical descent.

+ They were people of prayer and good works.
+ Both Joachim and Anne had been married for years; they were senior citizens.
  The birth of Mary was a fruit of grace rather than of nature.
+ Remember their girl Mary was immaculately conceived and sinless all her life.
+ Even though Joachim and Anne were outstanding parents, in God's plan the young girl needed more formation which her aged parents would have trouble giving her. The personnel in the temple were able to give Mary a higher quality education and upbringing. She lived there for eight years.
+ Again, according to the apocryphal material, Joachim died, and Anne had him buried in the Valley of Josaphat, not far from the Garden of Gethsemane. One year later, Anne rejoined her deceased husband there.
+ Mary returned home from the temple in Jerusalem to Nazareth and experienced the annunciation by Gabriel.

Saint Joseph's Mom and Dad, Jesus' Grandparents

Although in the Church we traditionally hold Joachim and Anne as the parents of Mary and the grandparents of Jesus, it is questionable they were alive when Jesus was born. We do know with certainty the name of the father of Saint Joseph, the foster father of Jesus.

In the genealogy of Jesus in Saint Matthew's Gospel, Joseph is listed as the son of "Jacob."[25] In the Gospel of Saint Luke, his father is listed as "Heli."[26]

Which is it? Was Joseph father Jacob or Heli? Jacob and Heli were half-brothers.

Heli died childless, so Jacob married his widow and fathered

---

[25] Matthew 1:16
[26] Luke 3:23

Joseph, who was biologically the son of Jacob but legally the son of Heli.[27] Therefore, this explains Saints Matthew and Luke.

The issue was adoption; it was a common in Jewish culture and, of course, that would affect genealogy. A person in one lineage, would take on a new lineage if he or she were adopted.

If a man died childless, it was the duty of his brother to marry the widow and father a son on behalf of his brother. I saw this during my time as a missionary in Kenya, East Africa.

Jacob was Joseph's primary father, the one who raised him up to be a "just man" as we read in sacred scripture.

A visionary from the 18th century, Mother Cecilia Baij, claims Joseph's mother was "Rachel." There is some possibility this could be true, as Rachel was and is a common name among the Jewish culture. We must be cautious: the visions of Mother Baij are "private revelation" and not authenticated by the Catholic Church.

---

[27] Eusebius, Ecclesiastical History, 1:6:7

Saint Padre Pio and
the Madonna

Saint Padre Pio is currently one of the best-loved saints in the Church today.

He had a deep devotion to the Madonna, as he called her. He prayed her Rosary daily and promoted its daily recitation to everyone.

I would like to share with you several quotes from Saint Padre Pio for your edification and inspiration.

> "Some people are so foolish that they think they can
> go through life without the help of the Blessed Mother.
> Love the Madonna and pray the Rosary, for her Rosary
> is the weapon against the evils of the world today.
> All graces given by God pass through the Blessed
> Mother."

> "Go to the Madonna. Love her! Always say the Rosary.
> Say it well.
> Say it as often as you can.
> Be souls of prayer. Never tire of praying.
> It is what is essential. Prayer shakes the heart of God,
> it obtains necessary graces."

> "The Rosary is the weapon for these times."

"Listen to the Mass the way the Virgin Mary stood at Calvary."

"Do you not see the Madonna always besides the tabernacle?"

"Lean on the cross of Jesus as the Virgin did it, you will not be deprived of comfort.

Mary was as if paralyzed before her crucified Son, but one cannot say that she was abandoned by him. Rather how much more did she not love him when she suffered and could not even weep?"

Do Whatever He Tells You

Mary does not say much in sacred scripture, but when she does, we need to stop and do what she did: ponder.

At Cana, Mary tells the servants of the catering service:

"Do whatever he tells you."

She herself did not know what to do, but she knew who did. Jesus knew what he was going to do; he was going provide more wine for all the guests. That did not mean going out to a vintner.

"Do whatever he tells you."

The "he" that Mary refers to is her Son Jesus. What the servants did not know: they were going to take part in Jesus' first miracle. It would be to save the young married couple from embarrassment, thanks be to the observance and charity of his Mother, their guest.

"Do whatever he tells you," and they did, and we know the consequences.

When we do whatever he tells us, we are doing the will of God in our lives.

As Saint Vincent de Paul tells his followers:

"Who is the most perfect of all human beings?
It will be the one whose will is most in conformity
with that of God, with the result that perfection (i.e.,

holiness) consists in uniting our will so closely in that of God that, strictly speaking, his and ours are only one and the same will and non-will…"[28]

When I recite the Luminous Mysteries and meditate on the fourth mystery "The Transfiguration" I relate the words of Mary's words at Cana: "Do whatever he tells you." And on the Mount Tabor, Abba says: "This is my Son, my Chosen, listen to him."[29]

"Do whatever he tells you" and "listen to him." Fabulous advice from Abba Father and the Mother of Jesus

---

[28] CCD, Vol. 11, #143, October 17, 1655
[29] Luke 9: 35

The Mary I Knew as a Youth

As a youth growing up in Chicago at Our Lady of Grace Parish on the northwest side, initially I knew two other Blessed Mothers: Our Lady of Sorrows and Our Lady of Lourdes. Later, a small statue of Our Lady of Fatima appeared on a table in the sanctuary. That totaled four Marys.

I knew very little about any of the four, but I loved our "lower church" where the back wall of the sanctuary was constructed of slabs of stone with a niche from which Our Lady of Lourdes looked out at us. There was a stirring within me of an affection for the Blessed Mother. Here I discovered my spiritual Mother.

While attending high school conducted by the Vincentians, I learned that there was another significant Blessed Mother: Our Lady of the Miraculous Medal.

On a trip to Perryville, Missouri, at fifteen years old, I saw the shrine of Our Lady of the Miraculous Medal for the first time. It was a "wow experience." I made up my mind: if I became a priest, I promised God and Mary that I would celebrate my first private Mass at the shrine altar.

I fulfilled the promise the day after ordination. In attendance were my stepdad (my mom had died two years before ordination), my brother and sisters, and family guests.

During the coming years, whenever I returned to our Vincentian seminary at Perryville for a meeting, I would make it my business to visit the shrine and pray to Our Lady. Now, I am retired within two minutes walking distance from the shrine. God is good.

Around my neck, 24/7, is her Miraculous Medal. Mary told us to wear it that way, although I also have a medal in my rosary pouch.

Mary is my life, my sweetness, and my hope. She is my Mother. Who is she for you?

The Old Man on the Train

There is a charming old story that you may have heard in the pulpit or read in a book. It is a good one for our edification and inspiration.

A somewhat arrogant university student boarded a train in France and sat down next to an older man who seemed like nothing out of the ordinary. The brash university student noticed that the older gentleman was slipping beads through his fingers. He was praying the Rosary.

"Sir, do you still believe in such outdated things?"

"Yes, I do. Don't you?"

The student laughed.

"I don't believe in such a silly thing. Take my advice and throw that Rosary out the window. Learn what science has to say about it."

"Science? I do not understand this science. Perhaps you can explain it to me," the man said humbly, tears welling in his eyes.

The university student noticed that the man was deeply moved. To his credit, the student did have some sensitivity; he did not want to hurt the man's feelings any further.

"Please give me your address, and I will send you some
literature to explain the matter to you."

The old man fumbled in his pocket and pulled out a business
card. On reading it, the student lowered his head in shame and was
speechless.

The card read: "Louis Pasteur, Director of the Institute of
Scientific Research, Paris."

The deluded university science student had just sat in the presence
of one greatest chemists and bacteriologists the world has ever known.

If Louis Pasteur said the Rosary, can we?

We Cannot Forget
What the Rosary Is

"When we recite the Rosary, we are stepping into the domain of Mary, a place of holy tranquility, a well-ordered world where we meet familiar images, where we find roads that lead us to the essential."[30]

Although the Rosary is Marian in character, it is at heart Christ-centered.

The Rosary has all the depth of the gospel message in its entirely (the combined four mysteries).[31]

"The Rosary is the means given us by the Blessed Virgin Mary to contemplate Jesus…we may love and follow him ever more faithfully."[32]

The Rosary is an effective weapon against the evils afflicting society throughout the world.[33]

For many Christians, the Rosary is their favorite prayer – a comfort in the early light of dawn or at 2 am in the darkness of a sleepless night. The Rosary is surely available morning, noon, and night. I usually pray the Rosary around 6 am.

Anyone can pray the Rosary because of its simplicity of composition, yet it plunges us into the depth of God's love.

While reciting of the words of the "Hail Mary," we meditate on the principal events in the life of our Lord and Savior Jesus Christ and

---

[30] A few thoughts from a great Msgr. Romano Guardini (+1968)
[31] Marialis Cultus, Pope Saint Paul VI, February 2, 1974, #42
[32] Angelus, Pope Benedict XVI, October 7, 2007
[33] Supremi Apostolatus Officio, Pope Leo XIII, 1884. 280289

our Mother Mary. These events come to life within the four mysteries of the Rosary: joyful, sorrowful, luminous, and glorious.

To pray the Rosary is nothing more than to contemplate with Mary the face of Jesus as I mentioned above.

It would be impossible to identify the countless saints who saw the Rosary as a genuine means for their growth in holiness of life. The same truth holds for the women and men that I have met throughout the United States, Canada, Kenya, and elsewhere in my life as a priest who replicates the same option of the saints.

****

As I mentioned, I pray the Rosary every day. This was not always the case in my earlier priesthood.

During that time, I said the Rosary at wake services or when a parish program necessitated it.

Now, when a priest and I are traveling up or down Interstate 55, we put on a Rosary disc and pray it together. Often, on Sundays, I will say it in conjunction with the Rosary said on Sirius Radio channel #129 preceding Mass at St. Patrick's Cathedral, New York. This was what I had been doing during the pandemic.

From my conversations with various priests, the Rosary is not for everyone. That is the reality. But many do have a strong relationship with Mother Mary, e.g., they are faithful to weekly novena prayers or they pray to Our Lady for themselves or for some purpose or persons in their lives.

I have discovered that the Rosary has helped me to fall deeper in love with Mother Mary, who, in turn, has brought me closer to her Son. I am more than grateful.

That is my hope for you.

> "May the Mother of Jesus, and our Mother, always
> smile on you and obtain for you, from her Most Holy
> Son, every heavenly blessing." (Saint Padre Pio)

The Hail Mary Has a History

We know the prayer as The Hail Mary or the Ave Maria or The Angelic Salutation or The Salutation of the Blessed Virgin Mary. How many times have we said it?

By whatever name we know it, the prayer has a history. The prayer stems from two passages from the Gospel of Saint Luke:[34]

> "Hail, full of grace, the Lord is with you"
> and
> "Blessed are you among women and blessed is the fruit of your womb!"

These two verses from St. Luke are the earliest form of the Hail Mary and was first recorded as being used by Pope Gregory the Great (509-604 AD). He ordered that the short prayer be recited as the Offertory of the Mass, fourth Sunday of Advent.

Under Pope Urban IV (1261-1264), the name of Jesus was added to the prayer. Mary's name was added sometime previously. The version was then: "Hail Mary, full of grace, the Lord is with you. Blessed are you among women and blessed is the fruit of your womb, Jesus."

The final additions to the prayer were made during early fourteen century. In 1508, "Holy Mary, pray for us sinners" was added with "now and at the hour of our death" used by some traditions, not

---

[34] Luke 1:28 and Luke 1:42

all. By 1515, the prayer that we know today became widespread in Western Europe.

The Hail Mary is the backbone of the Rosary; we say it 53 times in comparison to the Our Father said only 6 times.

It is possible the Rosary predated the Hail Mary prayer. Some scholars hold that the rosary began simply as a way for monks to keep track of the prayers they were saying, e.g., the 150 psalms daily.

The Ave Maria was only officially finalized when the Catechism of the Council of Trent was published in 1566.

This Catechism defines the two parts:

It calls the Hail Mary the Angelical Salutation.

1. When we pray 'Hail Mary, full of grace, the Lord is with you, blessed are thou among women,' we are rendering to God the highest praise and return him most grateful thanks, because he accumulated all his heavenly gifts on the most Holy Virgin; the Virgin herself, for this her singular felicity, we present our respectful and fervent congratulations.
2. To this form of thanksgiving the church of God has wisely added…an invocation of the most holy Mother of God, by which we piously and humbly fly to her patronage, in order that, by interposing her intercession, she may conciliate the friendship of God to us miserable sinners, and may obtain for us those blessings which we stand in need of in this life and in the life to come…

The Hail Mary remains a very important prayer for Catholics all over the world. It is a great expression of love for the Virgin Mary using words of Sacred Scripture itself.

There are three key values that we can learn from Mary that she fully practiced in her life: humility, simplicity, and charity. These three values are the same values lived out in the lives of the Daughters of Charity of St. Vincent de Paul.

They are the three virtues also practiced by the Ladies of Charity and other members of the Vincentian Family.

These three values – virtues – are important in all our lives.

The World's Most Famous Woman

Too many have placed Mary, Mother of Jesus, on a tall pedestal and made her unreachable. I first heard this remark from a married woman in the front parlor of Saint Vincent de Paul Church, Chicago when I was associate pastor (now called parochial vicar).

If anything, Mary is reachable and wants to be reachable to her children. Over the years, people have experienced her reachability.

Consider the facts:

Our Lady has inspired more art and music than any other woman in the history of humankind.

Mary holds the co-record with Princess Diana on appearances of the cover of TIME magazine eight times. On the December 30, 1991, the cover read: "The Search for Mary." In the years since, many have found their treasure!

We have problems, grave ones, but remember Mary lived under Roman occupation forces. She knew what it was like in the village of Nazareth. She heard Joseph and Jesus talk about the social and political issues prevalent at the time.

Something we forget: Mary was a Jewish woman, a wife, a mother; she changed diapers, cuddled Jesus, burped Jesus, rocked him to sleep. She laughed, cried; she cooked, did laundry, swept floors, walked to the common well for water. She fell asleep in a chair Joseph had made for her after a long day in and out of the house.

There is no way in the world to know the number of books and articles in periodicals on Mary. The same applies to the number of homilies by the clergy about her. It applies also to the number of workshops on Our Lady by religious and laity.

Mary must hold first place of all women ever born or will be.

Growing up as the oldest of seven, I am aware that a mother has a unique perspective. Often in my pre-teens I reaped the benefit of my mother's words of wisdom, often coming out of nowhere. As my mother had been a professional dancer in show business, I believe that she shared some of the "street-smarts" that she had learned from her travels with women and men of the dance group throughout the states.

Jesus had to have benefited from his Mother's street wisdom during his preteens and early adulthood.

The main reason why Mary is the famous of all women: she is "theokotus" – "God-bearer." Mary is the Mother of Jesus, and Jesus is God. Therefore, Mary is the Mother of God.

> "Hail Mary…blessed is the fruit of thy womb, Jesus.
> Holy Mary, Mother of God, pray for us sinners.
> Now and at the hour of our death. Amen."

****

I have been blessed to help with the ministry of The Association of the Miraculous Medal here at the National Shrine, Perryville, Missouri. I am flabbergasted at the snail and electronic mail that pours into the office from all over the world. People requesting Masses to be said, asking us to pray for various intentions, to have votive candles be lighted at the shrine. People love Our Lady!

Mary and the Man She Loved

Too often, we place the little statues of Mary and Joseph in the nativity scene for Christmas, but are they not lifeless? We need to remember that Mary and Joseph were real human beings with emotions like our own, with dreams like our own, with concerns like our own.

They were two people in love!

Joseph was the man Mary loved. They got married in a Jewish ceremony. It was not a typical marriage: Mary and Joseph did not consummate their marriage. As Catholics, we believe that Mary was a virgin before, during, and after the birth of her Son Jesus.

Joseph and Mary were without a doubt husband and wife. Mary found her soul mate: one who shared her moral principles and spiritual values as illustrated by the presentation of Jesus in the temple. Joseph and Mary met two extraordinary people there: Simeon and Anna.

It took four days for Mary and Joseph to make the trip from Nazareth to Jerusalem. Wanting to fulfill what the Jewish law prescribed, they found their joyful celebration turn bittersweet by the words of Simeon:

> "This child is destined for the falling and the rising of
> many in Israel, a sign that will be opposed.…
> a sword will pierce your own soul too."[35]

---

[35] Luke 2: 34-35

From the first day of their life together, Mary and Joseph worked at unity in their marriage, as you who are married know what I am talking about. Marriage is stronger when the two of you face everything together.

We know that Joseph and Mary celebrated at least twelve years of married life as we see from the finding of the lost Jesus in the temple.[36]

Mary and Joseph trusted God, and they trusted each other. Mary trusted God as did Joseph, e.g., to marry a pregnant young woman. Joseph too trusted God to begin their marriage as a stepfather.

Joseph and Mary faced problems head on with faith, hope, and perseverance. For example, they faced being socially outcast due to Mary's pregnancy, giving birth to her child in a cave where animals stayed, the need to flee to a foreign country to escape the tyrant King Herod who wanted to kill the baby (and perhaps them too!), the relocation to a new community once back in their own country.

Their marriage was strong because they each were strong personalities with unique spiritual lives and because they faced every challenge together. They trusted God completely. We see Joseph following God's directives communicated in dreams.

They had to believe that God would not allow anything to happen to his only begotten Son.

Those of you who are married is your trust in God and in each other strong?

Those of you who are single or had been married, is your trust in God strong and in your other relationships?

****

One of my favorite holy cards is called "Mary Resting."[37]

In the background Mary is on the bed sound to sleep exhausted

---

[36] Luke 2:48

[37] St. Joseph Guild, Flourtown, Pa.

from taking care of the baby all night. Saint Joseph is holding the baby in his arms.

Many of us pray to Saint Joseph for a happy death. I highly recommend it.

Can you imagine the happy death Joseph had with Mary and the teen Jesus by his bedside?

Our Lady of.........
(You fill in the blank)

I talk and write much about Blessed Antoine-Frederic Ozanam. He was married and father of a daughter. He is one of my prime heroes.

This man had a remarkable devotion to Our Lady. Wherever he traveled, he found a shrine of Mary and prayed there. He usually writes about the occasion as evidenced in his vast correspondence.

The year before he died, he visited the Spanish city of Burgos, and in the ancient cathedral he was deeply moved by Our Lady of Burgos on the main altar. I have prayed there myself and know something of what he shares.

> "Ah, Holy Virgin my Mother who are a powerful Lady! And in return for your poor house in Nazareth where you housed your divine Son, how many wonderful mansions has he given you.

> "O, Our Lady of Burgos who are also Our Lady of Pisa and of Milan, Our Lady of Cologne and of Paris, of Amiens and of Chartres, Rome...yes, truly 'You are beautiful and gracious...Good Virgin, you have obtained miracles, obtain something for us also and for those belonging to us.

Strengthen this fragile and broken-down dwelling of
our bodies. Cause the spiritual building of our souls
to rise up to heaven."[38]

We have heard, read, and personally experienced so many infirmed
as a result of Covid-19, thousands of deaths throughout the world,
millions of the unemployed, thousands of children learning in virtual
classrooms, health care professionals risking their lives to serve their
sisters and brothers, churches of every domination closed and the list
goes on.

During all of this, we lift our voice to Our Lady (put in the name
of your city, church, family.…).

We cry out to Our Lady of_____ to be a Mother of
Love to us, to our loved ones, to our city, to our nation. Mary, our
life, our sweetness, and our hope.…

---

[38] L # 1191, Charles Ozanam. November 18-19, 1852. Also, in the Book of the Sick,
Frederic Ozanam, p. 32.

Happy Birthday![39]

On September 8th, we celebrate the birthday of the Blessed Virgin Mary. Nine months ago, in December, we commemorated her Immaculate Conception.

We do not possess absolute creditable information about the infancy and early life of Mary; sacred scripture does not furnish us with such information.

The "Protoevangelium of James" (early second century) provides data on Our Lady's father and mother.

We honor our Mother Mary even more than other saints for one simple reason: she is the Mother of our Lord Jesus Christ, our Savior who is a Person of the Holy Trinity: Father, Son, and Holy Spirit.

Saint Augustine has described the birth of Mary as an event of cosmic and historic significance and an appropriate prelude to the birth Our Lord Jesus. As he said:

> "Through her birth, the nature inherited from our
> first parents is changed."

In celebrating this birthday of Our Lady, we would do well to reflect or ponder on the life which Mary had led, her commitment and total surrender to God's will when she said "Yes" to God through the Archangel Gabriel.

---

[39] The Catholic Church celebrates three birthdays in its liturgical year: Jesus (Christmas Day), Mary (September 8), and John the Baptist, Precursor (June 24)

Mary continuously shows us the way forward in our spiritual life.

The birth of Our Lady has brought hope to the whole world. Because of her, we can gaze on the face of her Son, who is the Way, the Truth, and the Life.

Our Lady of the Grapes

The 44th parallel is a prime growing area for grapes used for wine. In France and other grape-growing countries, a traditional harvest blessing of grapes is held on Mary's birthday, September 8th. In areas of Wisconsin, this also is a special day.

The French vintners call this feast "Our Lady of the Grape Harvest."

In the Beaujolais wine region, there is a church called La chapel Notre-Dame-aux-Raisins. Each year on this day in the region, vintners make a pilgrimage to the church atop Mount Brouilly with their best grapes from the early harvest. The grapes are blessed and then bunches are placed into the hands of Mary's statues.

The vintners discovered years ago to place their grapes into the hands of Mary!

A picnic lunch with a good bottle of wine follows.

Italians eat blueberries on Mary's birthday. The blue of the berry reminds every one of the traditional color of Mary's outer garment. Lights are lighted in windows.

Many places light bonfires on this night.

In Austria, sheep and cattle are brought down the mountains into valleys before winter hits. Mary's Birthday is known there as "Drive Down Day." After a celebration, in some places, milk and leftovers are given to the poor in honor of Our Lady's birthday.

There is No Room in the Inn

There was no room in the local inn for the pregnant Mary and her husband Joseph. Both were exhausted after a grueling trip from Nazareth to Bethlehem especially since she was nine months pregnant, so close to giving birth.

They would have traveled ninety miles along the flatlands of the River Jordan, then west over the hills surrounding the city of Jerusalem, and on into Bethlehem.

As the mileage at the time was usually ten miles a day, Joseph and Mary probably did not go further because of Mary's condition.

The trip during the winter would indeed be grueling: thirty-degree temperatures with a good amount of rain; the night would be freezing. They would have dressed in heavy garments.

The unpaved, hilly paths and harsh weather was only part of the hazards.

The heavily wooden valley of the River Jordan had wild animals like bears and wild boars always seeking food. Archaeologists have discovered documents warning travelers of these dangers lurking in the forest areas.

Perhaps the more threatening hazard were the bandits hiding in the desert area. They attacked both individuals and caravans on the major trade routes like the one Joseph and Mary would have taken for companionship and protection.

Mary and Joseph had to bring sufficient food for the trip, certainly enough for ten days. That meant water in wineskins and plenty of unleavened bread. Breakfast and an afternoon snack would be bread with oil and bread and herbs with oil for an evening meal. The bread would be more like pita than another type.

As there was no room for them in the inn, in desperation they ended up in a stable.

It would have been dirty, smelly, and noisy.

Did Joseph find a midwife in time for Mary? There is no mention in sacred scripture about this.

Is there room for Mary and Joseph in the inn of your hearts? Do you inspire others in word and action? How do you feel about the homeless situation in our country?

Do you speak words of hope?

Jesus' Third Word from the Cross[40]

As Jesus hung dying on the cross, amid intense pain and suffering, he struggles with the last ounce of physical strength to get his last words heard to the two standing nearby: his loving Mother Mary and his beloved friend John. Both are sobbing with tears flowing down their cheeks.

The word of God is act. The Son of God in his dripping blood, sweating, and secreting bodily fluids delivers the mandate to his mother:

"Woman, here is your son."[41]

Jesus turns his blood-soaked hair and thorn-pierced head toward John:

"Here is your mother."[42]

In his last will and testament, the Son gifts us with a present that only a divine Son could give: his Mother who gave him birth, nursed him, raised him from infancy to adulthood, the Mother par excellence.

People usually bequeath their family money, property, heirlooms, whatever in their last wills and testaments, but Jesus is unique. He leaves us a gift of flesh and blood, his Mother, perhaps then a women of forty-eight years old.

---

[40] This second of Jesus 7 last words.
[41] John 19:27
[42] Ibid.

Jesus gifts humankind with the woman who knew only love. Every act of Mary was an act of love. In today's time, every act of Mary is the same: love. We see this time and again in every apparition of Mary, wherever she appears, in any country, to any person. Love is an active verb, not a noun.

In every apparition, Mary is faithful to the mandate given her from the cross.

In every case, Mary manifests a mother's love, gifts people with inspiration and hope.

Miriam of Nazareth

May I offer a suggestion?

Use your imagination: consider Mary as Miriam of Nazareth. She is a teenager living in a backwater village of Galilee of about 400 citizens.[43]

Miriam was a common name given to girls by their Hebrew parents. Perhaps given in memory of Miriam, the sister of Moses and Aaron, two giants in Jewish history!

This girl Miriam is chosen by God while young, between the age of 13-15, to become the mother of the Messiah!

Too often in paintings, even by extraordinary artists, we see Mary pictured in a luxurious setting, dressed in gorgeous garments. I must believe that this is the furthest from reality.

Miriam was probably sweeping the dirt floor of the small home, or perhaps doing laundry, or maybe preparing pita, when suddenly out of nowhere appeared a powerful looking person that we know as the Archangel Gabriel. He was certainly not ordinary looking. In Hebrew, Gabriel means "God is my strength" or "God is my strong man."

Gabriel appears and greets this Miriam not by her name but by the phrase "Hail, full of grace." Gabriel knows who she is! Was he not calling by her "heavenly name?" Gabriel had appeared previously to

---

[43] A recent census lists Nazareth with a population of 77, 495. It is called "The Arab capital of Israel."

Zechariah, an extraordinary person, but now he meets Miriam, the holiest human being ever created by God.

Gabriel's sudden appearance had to startle her! He says, "no fear."[44] Miriam did not know his name until later. All she knew: an angel suddenly was in front of me and had something to say. Gabriel was all business; there was no small talk.

Gabriel revealed God's plan to the young teen. What is the first thing we hear from Miriam? An expression of confusion. "How can this be since I am a virgin?

The archangel provides essentials. We hear about the power of the Holy Spirit, who, at that time, Mary did not have a clue who that was. Gabriel is talking about the third Person of the Holy Trinity even before Jesus' birth!

The young Miriam is the first person in sacred scripture introduced to Holy Spirit who will overshadow her, and she will become pregnant with the Son of God.

That had to impact on her! Here was a girl who practiced purity.

I must believe that Miriam immediately told her parents that she was now pregnant. How do they believe this? They know the truthfulness and goodness of their daughter. She tells them the whole story about her conversation with God's angel.

They hear that their innocent daughter was going to become the mother of the Messiah who the Jewish people have been waiting for centuries. That is indeed an incredible story that they heard from Miriam!

What about her engagement with Joseph? She needed to talk to him right away!

She told her parents about Elizabeth's pregnancy that no one could know. At that time, Miriam asked permission to go and assist Elizabeth and Zechariah because of their advanced age. Miriam was not bound by justice but went because of charity. This mode of action is something to consider for everyone.

---

[44] This is what the Greek text says. The usual translation is: "Do not be afraid."

Miriam's father booked passage for her with a trade caravan. Did this young girl go by herself or did she have a companion? I must believe that somebody went with her. Miriam was a young teen and now pregnant! I suppose that Joseph could not leave the carpenter shop for any length of time.

She stayed three months and then returned home. Miriam was now four months pregnant.

What charity from a young teen, but what maturity!

Scapulars Come in Colors

Scapulars, devotional scapulars, are objects of popular piety.

The scapular typically consists of two rectangular pieces of cloth connected by bands. [I have a new Brown Scapular with bands made of a thin leatherette material.] One rectangle rests on the upper chest, while the other rests on the upper back, with the bands running over the shoulders.

Scapulars come in various colors according to their spiritual intent: white, black, brown, red, green, and blue are the dominant colors. When bunched together, they form a variegated bouquet for Mother Mary and her Son, Jesus!

I dare say that the Brown Scapular was and is the more famous of all scapulars. I remember receiving one at my First Communion along with a small prayer book. I do not know if that is being the case anymore today in parishes on a national basis.

The Brown Scapular

The Scapular of Our Lady of Mount Carmel is the correct name for the Brown Scapular. The scapular is silent prayer. One member of the hierarchy has called it "a constant meditation."

Tradition tells us that the Blessed Mary appeared to Saint Simon Stock at Aylesford, England in 1251 and gave him the Brown Scapular (designated for the Carmelite habit). The exact origin is debated, but the Brown Scapular has been part of the Carmelite habit since the late 13th century.

The Blessed Virgin Mary of Mt. Carmel has promised to save those who wear the scapular from the fires of hell or shorten their stay in purgatory if it is necessary.

Our Lady of Mount Carmel feast day is July 26th.

The Red Scapular

The Red Scapular of the Passion of Our Lord and the Sacred Hearts of Jesus and Mary is a popular devotional for many.

Sister Apolline Andriveau, a Daughter of Charity of St. Vincent de Paul, was the recipient of visions of Jesus and Mary from July 26 to September 14, 1846. She had these visions in her convent at Troyes, France. Jesus and Mary promised that those who wear the red scapular faithfully and contemplated the passion of Jesus would be granted a great increase of faith, hope, and charity every Friday.

The Sister described her visions in specific and vivid details. She also described a scene reminiscent of the Pieta:

> "One Sunday evening, I was making the Stations of the Cross. At the 13th Station, it seemed to me that our Blessed Lady placed the Body of our Divine Lord in my arms….'The world is drawing down ruin upon itself because it never thinks of the Passion of Jesus Christ. Do your utmost to bring it to meditate thereon, to bring about its salvation."

On the eve of octave of the Feast of Saint Vincent de Paul,[45] Sister Apolline had a vision of Jesus:

---

[45] July 26, 1846. The feast is now September 27th.

"....clad in a long red robe and blue mantle. Oh! Love of Jesus Christ, how you filled my heart at that moment! How beautiful he was! It was no longer the painful expression...It was beauty itself! In his right hand he held a scapular upon which was a crucifix surrounded by those instruments of the Passion which caused his sacred humanity to suffer most. I read around the crucifix: 'Holy Passion of Our Lord Jesus Christ, protect us.' At the other end of the red woolen braid was a picture of the Sacred Hearts of Jesus and Mary, one surrounded with thorns, the other pierced by a lance, and both surrounded by a cross."

Sister Apolline described other visions, one on the Feast of the Holy Trinity in which she saw a beautiful river representing Christ's mercy in which those immersed glowed with bright light and "sheaves of diamonds and gold," while those refusing immersion "were covered with a dark vapor."

Pope Pius IX approved the use of the sacramental on June 25, 1857.

The Green Scapular

The Green Scapular is also called "The Badge of the Immaculate Heart of Mary."

This devotional was approved by Pope Pius IX in 1870.

Sister Justine Bisqueyburu, a Daughter of Charity of St. Vincent de Paul, had a vision in 1840 that led to the creation of the Green Scapular.

The Blessed Mother appeared to Sister Justine on January 28, 1840 during her retreat in preparation for entrance into the Daughters of Charity in the same Parisian chapel where Our Lady had appeared to St. Catherine Laboure in July ten years before. Mary said nothing to Sister Justice at this time.

The Blessed Virgin appeared again to Sister Justine at the end of the retreat and five times during Sister's novitiate. The vision was identical to the first; Our Lady said nothing.

On September 8, 1840, the Feast of Mary's Birthday, the Virgin Mary appeared to Sister Justine at prayer. Our Lady was holding her heart surrounded by flames in her right hand, and in her left, a type of scapular consisting of a single piece of green cloth strung on green cords. On the cloth was an image of her as she had appeared to Sister Justine, holding her heart in her right hand. On the reverse was "a heart all ablaze with rays more dazzling than the sun and as transparent as crystal."

The heart was pierced by a sword, surmounted by a gold cross and the words in the shape of an oval around the heart: "Immaculate Heart of Mary, pray for us now and at the hour of our death."

Sister told her superior and spiritual director Jean-Marie Aladel, C.M. (the same priest to whom Saint Catherine Laboure had told of her visions in 1830!) Sister Justine had heard an interior voice that Our Lady wished the scapular to be promoted widely as an instrument in the conversions of souls.

In 1867, Sister Justine went to Rome to equip three ambulances for her ministry in military hospitals. She became friendly with Pope Pius IX and, at times, walked with him in the papal gardens.

Pope Pius IX approved the Green Scapular in 1870.

Isn't it amazing that the Blessed Virgin Mary appeared to three different Daughters of Charity in the same chapel of Paris? Is not the fact that she appeared to Sisters of the same community truly remarkable? No wonder the chapel of rue du Bac is so awe-inspiring! I love the chapel and have enjoyed praying there.

The Blue Scapular

The Blue Scapular originated in Naples, Italy in 1617. Our Lady Mary appeared to Ursula Benincasa who had founded the Congregation of the Oblates of the Immaculate Conception of the Most Blessed Virgin Mary in 1883. The Sisters have been called "The Theatines" or "The Theatine Nuns."

On the Feast of the Presentation of the Lord, after having received Holy Communion, the Blessed Mother appeared to Sister Ursula in a white garment over which was another garment of azure blue. In her arms she held the infant Jesus. Surrounding Mary were many persons attired in the same habit.

> "Cease weeping, Ursula, and turn your sighs into heartfelt joy.
>
> Listen closely to what Jesus, whom I am holding in my lap, will say to you."

Jesus revealed to Ursula that she would found a convent where 33 nuns, dressed in the same habit as Our Lady in her vision, and would live a life of solitude and seclusion. The Savior promised special graces and spiritual gifts to those who followed this way of life with great zeal.

Sister Ursula asked Jesus to extend these favors also to those in the world with a special devotion to the Immaculate Conception, observe chastity according to their vocation in life, and wear a small blue scapular.

As a sign that her prayer request had been heard and granted, Jesus showed a scene in a fresco at the Theatine Sisters' convent in Naples.

Overcome with joy, Ursula personally made scapulars after the vision and gave them out to the faithful. The practice of wearing the Blue Scapular spread quickly.

After Ursula's death in 1618, her Sisters undertook the promotion of the scapular as their special mission.

The Theatine Fathers began promoting devotion of the Scapular of the Immaculate Conception of the Blessed Virgin Mary, a ministry assigned to their community by Pope Clement X on January 30, 1671.

The Holy Father endowed the scapular with many indulgences. These were confirmed and amplified by Pope Gregory XIV in 1845 and Pope Pius IX in 1850. Both popes declared that the indulgences of the Blue Scapular could be applied to the souls of the faithful departed.

Those who wear the Scapular of the Immaculate Conception can receive a Plenary Indulgence on the day of investiture with the scapular of the Immaculate Conception, on December 8, August 15, Christmas Day, February 2, Easter Sunday, the Ascension, August 7 (Feast of Saint Cajetan, founder of the Theatine Order.

As we see in these four scapulars of different colors, Our Lady promises love and hope.

****

I personally wear a scapular medal that I received from a dying priest who was a dear friend of mine. Father Joe is one reason I wear it, but not the only reason!

On December 16, 1910, Pope Saint Pius X approved the scapular medal as a substitute for any of the various cloth scapulars. A valid enrollment in the cloth scapular must be made before the substitution.

The medal must have an image of the Most Holy Redeemer, Jesus Christ, showing his Sacred Heart and on the reverse side that of the Blessed Virgin Mary.

The Second Annunciation

On Calvary, in midst of his intense suffering and pain, Jesus entrusted to John the apostle what was most precious to him: his Mother Mary. At times of death, often people express their deepest desires; Jesus certainly did.

At the Annunciation, Mary gave her DNA to the Son of God; at the foot of the cross, she becomes the Mother of humanity before the final moments.

Mary's "yes" to God through the Archangel Gabriel was the first annunciation. Mary's "second annunciation" occurred when her Son said to his sorrowful Mother: "Woman, here is your son."[46]

Jesus gives his Mother to comfort you and me with her incomparable mother's love and compassion

Saint John tells us that "from that hour the disciple took her to his own home."[47]

Have you taken Mary into your home? Have you welcomed her as one of the family?

As a member of your household, she will teach you and yours much. As your mother, you can expect a mother's love.

---

[46] John 19:26. Saint Pope John Paul II talked about the "second annunciation" in the 18th World Youth Day, March 19, 2003. It is a thought worth pondering.
[47] John 19:27

A Conversation

There are certain places that are holy because what occurred in them or because of who lived in them (I am not referring to a church or chapel). Such a special place is the rectory of Ars, France, where the Cure of Ars, Pere Jean-Marie Vianney, lived.

[I have read this story in the biographies of Saint Jean-Marie Vianney several times as well as hearing it in the retreat talk of Father Frederick I. Miller.[48] What a relationship Saint Jean-Marie had! It sounds like something from fiction, something too good to be true. I have never forgotten this story, especially during the two times I have visited Ars.]

Jean-Marie Vianney's birthday was May 8th. Miss Etiennette Durie visited parishioners and arrived at the rectory to drop off the gift offerings. It was one o'clock in the afternoon.

Catherine Lassagne, who oversaw the rectory, directed Miss Durie to upstairs.

As she ascended the staircase, she heard Pere Jean-Marie's voice talking to someone. There was a very gentle woman's voice:

"What do you ask?"
"Ah! My good Mother, I ask for… (Pere Jean-Marie listed a few things, all pastoral in nature).

---

[48] The Grace of Ars, Father Frederick I. Miller, Ignatius Press, 2010, pp.107-108

The woman replied:

"She will get well, but a little later."

Miss Durie slowly opened the door, which was already ajar,

> "Standing by the fireplace was a lady of ordinary height, clad in a robe of dazzling white, scattered with golden roses. Her shoes seemed to be white as snow, her fingers shone with the brightest of diamonds. Around her head was a wreath of stars shining like the sun. I was dazzled by their brilliance.
>
> When I could lift my eyes to hers, I saw her smile gently, "My good Mother," I exclaimed, "do take me with you to heaven."
>
> "Later on."[49]
>
> "Ah, my Mother, Now is the time."
>
> "You will always be my child, and I shall always be your Mother."

The lady vanished, leaving Jean-Maire standing with his hands pressed against his chest. His face was radiant, and his gaze fixed. Miss Durie tugged at his cassock. He looked at her.

> "What did you see?
> "A lady."
> "I too. Who is she?"

---

[49] Miss Durie had cancer.

"If you speak of it, you will never again set foot in this room."
"May I tell you what I thought, Pere? I thought it was our Lady."

The Cure grinned a little: "And you were not mistaken. So, you have seen her."[50]

[50] The Cure D'Ars Today Saint John Vianney, George William Rutler, Ignatius Press, 1988, pp. 205-206. I have used two different conversations for this dialogue. I think Father Miller's is a more accurate one.

The Color Green

Colors in our church's liturgical year are more than decoration or to brighten the church. They symbolize something in their "color-ness."

During those weeks known as "Ordinary Time," the color is green. The green vestments of the bishop, priest, and deacon symbolize hope and life.

When we think of green, we think of Spring, of new life, and to what is happening in nature: fertility, hope. When we think of green, we think of summer: vacations, picnics, family events, the swimming pool, the beach, camping.

I was born years before The Muppets, but I deeply admired the work and creativity of Jim Hensen. He created "Kermit the Frog." Who can forget his song?

"It's Not Easy Being Green."[51]

Kermit sings:

> "But green's the color of Spring
> and green can be cool and friendly like."

It is not easy being a disciple of Jesus, and he tells us that straight out in the beginning of his public ministry. Jesus forever tells us the truth.

Mary was Jesus' first disciple. She believed in him; she loved him unconditionally.

---

[51] The song is written by Joe Raposo

Is our color green?
Do we manifest hope, a new day, a better day?
It is not easy being green.
Talk to Mother Mary.

The Most Beautiful Name
in All the World

Eight days after birth, her parents, Joachim and Anne, inspired by God, gave their daughter the name Miriam (or, as we know her today, Mary).

In the Old Testament, our Jewish brothers and sisters did not speak the Name of God as Yahweh. Why? Because it was holy. They rendered it great reverence.

Today, unfortunately, too many takes God's name in vain or use it carelessly.

The Name of God is holy. Saint Paul says so in his Letter to the Philippians.

> 'The name above every other name,
> That at the name of Jesus every knee should bend,
> In the heavens, on the earth, and under the earth,
> And every tongue proclaim: to the glory of God the
> Father,
> Jesus Christ is Lord!"[52]

Our Blessed in her Magnificat says"

"And holy is his name."[53]

---

[52] Philippians 2:10-11
[53] Luke 1:49

Mary too: her name is holy. We find out her name from Saint Luke the evangelist, not from the Archangel Gabriel; he refers to her heavenly name: "Hail, full of grace."

The very name of Mary is a prayer.

Saint Bernard of Clairvaux says:

> "O most holy Virgin Mary, your name is so sweet and admirable that one cannot say it without becoming inflamed with love toward God and toward you."

Richard of Saint Laurence states:

> "There is not such powerful help in any name, nor is there any other name given to men, after that of Jesus, from which so much salvation is poured forth upon men as from the name of Mary..."

Saint Bonaventure declares

> "That your name, O Mary, cannot be pronounced without bringing some grace to the one who does so devoutly."

Thomas a Kempis affirms:

> "That the devils fear the Queen of heaven to such a degree, that only on hearing her great name pronounced, they fly from one who does so as from a burning fire."

The Catechism of the Catholic Church teaches:

> "Everyone's name is sacred.
> The name is the icon of the person.

It demands respect as a sign of the dignity of the one who bears it."[54]

The Catechism says earlier in its text:

"A name expresses a person's essence and identity and the meaning of this person's life.
To disclose one's name is to make oneself known to others...."[55]

To put the above quotations in other words:

A name of a human being is not just a label. Our reverence for the person is reflected in the reverence for that person's name. One's name contain our personal identity and represent our mission – who and what we are to the world in which we live.

All of this fits the person of Mary.

Mary's name is sacred. Jesus "disclosed" her person on the cross to make her accessible to humankind until the end of the world.

Mary's name is one of honor. The principal reason: because the faithful of the Church praise Mary as the Mother of our Divine Savior, Jesus. As Mother of God (the Mother of Jesus, the Second Person of the Holy Trinity) she deserves our honor and respect.

Mary's name is holy. Because the very mention of her name reminds us of who she is. She is, as the Archangel Gabriel said: "Full of grace." She has been chosen by God for one of the most significant missions of the world.

Mary's name is maternal, because she is our Mother, whom Jesus, her Son, gave us before his last breathes on the cross.

Mary's name is one of a mother who responds to our needs,

---

[54] CCC # 2158
[55] Ibid., # 203

protects us from evil, and prays "for sinners now and at the hour of our death."

Saint Bernard said it loud and clear:

> "If she holds you, you will not fall.
> If she protects you, you need not fear."[56]

On the Feast of the Name of Mary, we pray:

> "Grant, we pray, almighty God,
> that, for all who celebrate the glorious Name
> of the Blessed Virgin Mary,
> she may obtain your merciful favor."

---

[56] Pope Benedicy XVI, at Heiligenkreuz Abbey. September 9, 2007.

Why Does Mary Have So Many Names, Titles, and Feasts?

Why? Why does Mary? That is a good question.

Why does Mary have so many names, titles, and feasts? As I mentioned earlier in the text, the Marian Meditation Walk so close to my residence, it alone contains thirteen different statues of Mary. All thirteen do have different names, titles, and feast days.

Who do we hold responsible for this? Should we point the finger at Mary, or to Jesus? After all, Jesus gave us Mary as our Mother. Obviously, she has taken her mission seriously! (Are we blessed!)

Should we blame her for doing too much for too many? Or, in the light of the recent pandemic, implore her to do more?

Mary is one. There are not more than one Mary. What she has done over the centuries is mind boggling!

If we take a good look at the vast number of Marian apparitions, we must admit: through Mary's appearances and conversations, the faithful have increased their faith, hope, and charity.

Many of these faithful have spread their devotion to others, family, and non-family, but people of similar belief. The same may be said of those religious families who have spread devotion among themselves as well as to others.

The Fruits of the Rosary: The Virtues

Each mystery of the Rosary has what I call a corresponding virtue. To say it in another way: each mystery highlights a particular virtue. Upon meditating on each mystery, we come to see how the virtue is related to the mystery and how this virtue may become a part of our life.

At one time, I personally only concentrated on virtues rather than the mysteries per se.

As we pray the Rosary and reflect upon each mystery, we ask Our Lady to pray with us so that we might grow in virtue to please and become more like her Son.

The greatest of all virtues is humility. Without humility, our pride will surface and prevent us from cultivating any other virtue. The founder of our community, Saint Vincent de Paul, promoted five virtues for us individually and corporately; humility was a primary one. Other saints have preached and taught the same.

Our Blessed Lady will guide us. With her, as our example, we pray humbly, and we understand that we have much to learn!

I pray that these virtues as specified may be of assistance for you!

Virtues of the Joyful Mysteries

Annunciation: Humility
Visitation: Love of Neighbor

Nativity of Jesus: Love of Poverty or Detachment
Presentation: Obedience
Finding Jesus in the Temple: Joy in Finding Jesus in our life

Virtues of the Sorrowful Mysteries

Agony in the Garden of Gethsemane: Sorrow for My Sin or Trust in God
Scourging at the Pillar: Purity
Crowning with Thorns: Courage
Carrying of the Cross: Patience or Perseverance in difficulties of life
Crucifixion: Forgiveness for others who have hurt us

Virtues of the Luminous Mysteries

Baptism of Jesus: Openness to the Holy Spirit
The Wedding of Cana: Mary's intercession or to Jesus through Mary
Proclamation of the Kingdom of Heaven and Repentance: Christian
Witness and Conversion in Our Life
The Holy Eucharist: Greater love for the Holy Eucharist in Our Life
or Adoration

Virtues of the Glorious Mysteries

Resurrection: Faith in the Risen Lord
Ascension: Hope
Descent of the Holy Spirit: Gifts of the Holy Spirit; Pentecost
(Birthday of the Church)
Assumption or Dormition of Mary: Grace of a Happy Death
Coronation of Our Lady: Final Perseverance to the End or Trust in
the Queen of Heaven and Earth

Decisions in the Rosary

One of the things that has struck me in recent years as I meditate on the Rosary is the momentous decisions made by Jesus and Mary in various Mysteries.

In our mediations on the Mysteries, we usually concentrate on the physical activity involved and overlook the decision made with its implications. Let me give four examples (there are others).

The Annunciation

We can focus on the Archangel Gabriel and Mary's conversation, and forget that Mary has not only said "Yes" to God, but said "No" to the plans that she had made: the big wedding, children, her spotless reputation among the citizens of Nazareth, ramifications on Joseph's life. He would be forced to make big decisions.

The Nativity

The decision divinely made by the Holy Trinity. It would change the world forever: the time was chosen: the young teen had been picked out from eternity, and she is physically ready to have a child. The Holy Trinity has decided: God will become human out of love to die out of love for the sins of humankind.

The Finding of the Child Jesus in the Temple

The twelve-year-old decides to remain back in Jerusalem. His Mother and foster father are worried to death, and Mary tells her Son what they feel.

Jesus says: "Did you not know that I had to be about my Father's business?" In our words, "I had to be about the Father's mission." The pre-teen had decided.

Jesus in the Garden of Gethsemane

Jesus sweats blood over the decision: to turn himself over to the authorities which means death. The time has come. His decision will involve mockery, severe pain, the loss of blood, and the Roman garrison's use of him as a play toy. He has decided to die in reparation for the sins of the world.

The Golden Hail Mary

Saint Gertrude the Great[57] was a German Benedictine, a friend of Saint Mechtild of Magdeburg who was her teacher. Gertrude was a mystic, a writer, and an intellectual.

Saint Gertrude was blessed with visions of Jesus.

One of the famous visions of Saint Gertrude was seeing Jesus in front of a tall pile of gold coins which were glimmering, glowing. If you can imagine, a pile of coins that sparked with beauty!

The saint saw Jesus to deposit another shining gold coin and place it on top of the other coins. This last coin seemed to glisten more than the others.

Saint Gertrude asked Jesus why the last coin he had deposited seemed to have had a special glimmer to it.

> "My daughter, every time you pray a calm, fervent,
> and loving Hail Mary to my Mother, I deposit a
> golden coin in the treasury of heaven for you."

I think that the interpretation of this vision is not complicated: Mary is the Mother of God, the Mother of the Church, and the Mother of each one of us.

Mary has a great maternal love for all of us and desires our happiness in this life and especially in the next. There is a prayer that causes the Immaculate Heart of Mary to rejoice: it is the Hail Mary!

---

[57] Saint Gertrude – 1250-1301

My recommendation: Take the Hail Mary, say it slowly, pondering each word, relishing each word, really savoring it to the fullest.

You and I have prayed thousands of the Hail Mary. It is a spiritual diamond, a spiritual masterpiece.

Perhaps, we can add a gold coin to Jesus' pile!

Mary, Did You Know?[58]

[Mary was probably between 13-15 years old when Jesus was born in Bethlehem.]

Mary, did you know as you held your Son in your arms, as you nursed him, as you changed his diapers, as you burped him, as you rocked him to sleep, when you had him circumcised, did you know?

Mary, did you know that you and your husband and your Son would have to flee for your lives to Egypt to escape death from Herod, that you had to depend upon others for existence during that time?

Mary, did you know when you presented your Son in the temple that he would be destined for the rising and falling of many in Israel, that he would be a sign of contradiction, that your own heart, your own soul, a sword would pierce?

Mary, did you know as you saw Jesus crawl for the first time, say "mama" for the first time, walk for the first time, ask to go to the potty for the first time?

Mary, did you know as you saw the little boy Jesus in the carpentry shop with Joseph playing on the floor, and later saw him playing in the street with other kids, did you know?

Mary, did you know when he started talking excellent Aramaic so quickly, when you took him to the synagogue, and he paid strict attention unlike other kids, did you know?

---

[58] "Mary, Did You Know" – songwriters Buddy Greene and Mark Lowry, Warner Chappell Music, Inc. This is one of my favorite Christmas songs! Its lyrics give us much food for pondering with Mary!

Mary, did you know when your Son grew up in excellent physical condition and take over the shop after Joseph died, that he would not marry a Jewish girl and be celibate?

Mary, did you know that your Son would one day leave the hidden life and go public?

Mary, did you know that your Son would walk on water, raise people from the dead, give sight to the blind, calm a storm on the Sea of Galilee?

Mary, did you know that you would see your Son covered with blood and crowned with thorns carrying a heavy beam of a cross through the Jerusalem streets to his death?

Mary, did you know that you would see your Son's stripped body nailed to a cross, suffer from excessive body cramps, and fight for breathes from asphyxiation?

Mary, did you know that you would be holding your Son's lifeless, limp body on your lap?

Mary, did you know that three days later you would be hugging your Risen Son in his glorified body?

Mary, did you know – any of this?

Mary and The Archbishop

One of my heroes in priesthood is the deceased Cardinal Francis Xavier Nguyen Van Thuan.

I heard him speak in Los Angeles at USC. In my opinion, he delivered one of the best talks that I have ever heard on Jesus. I sat there mesmerized. I said to myself: "This archbishop not only knows Jesus, but he also loves Jesus."

I have read his books "The Road of Hope" and "Five Loaves and Two Fish." They are in my bookcase.

I want to share with you a few thoughts from this latter book for your inspiration.

Archbishop Francis Xavier related that he had prayed at the grotto of Lourdes several times. From 1975, when he was arrested, and during the thirteen years of his confinement, he understood that the Madonna had been preparing him for years:

> "I do not promise you joy and consolation in this life, but trials and suffering." (Words of Mary to Saint Bernadette)

> "Every day I understood more intimately the deep meaning of this message, and I confidently abandoned myself into Mary's hands."[59]

---

[59] Five Loaves and Two Fish, Francis Xavier Nguyen Van Thuan, Pauline Books & Media, Boston, p. 63

One day, after years imprisoned, the archbishop was driven to meet the Minister of the Interior (i.e., the police). And he asked the archbishop:

"Do you have any desires to express?"

"Yes. I want my freedom."

"When?"

"Today."

And after some remarks from the archbishop, the Minister turned to his secretary:

"Do whatever is necessary to fulfill his request."
At that moment, the archbishop thought:
"Today is the feast of Mary's Presentation.
It is Mary who is setting me free. Thank you, Mary!"[60]

---

[60] Ibid. pp. 64-65

The Joyful Mysteries

[A few thoughts of mine that you may find helpful.]

The Joyful Mysteries are about beginnings (in order): of Mary, John the Baptist, Jesus, the Pre-teen Jesus.

The Annunciation

God is the God of surprises, of the unexpected.

The Archangel Gabriel, God's envoy, appears out of nowhere to the young teenager. He does not call her Miriam, her Hebrew name, but "Hail, full of grace." I see this as Mary's heavenly name, the name the angels know her by.

"Full of grace" – in Greek: "completely, perfectly, enduringly empowered with grace." In Greek, it is not just a description but a permanent state. Mary has been and always will be "full of grace."

Mary, in minutes, reinvents her life! Aren't many of us doing the same: reinventing our lives individually and corporately during this pandemic?

Mary is ageless. You and I pray to her as if she is fifteen, twenty-five, or forty-five. As we see in the apparitions, Mary appears in different "ages."

The Visitation

Mary, pregnant with Jesus for perhaps a month, makes a long tiring trip by caravan to Ein Karem to spend time with Elizabeth now six months pregnant with John. As an adult, people will nickname him "The Baptist."

Mary's trip is one of charity, not justice. She stays three months with the couple and returns home. Mary is now four months pregnant herself. I imagine that the return trip to Nazareth had to be physically more grueling for her.

The Nativity

After nine months, Jesus is born in Bethlehem. There is no room for them in an inn.

Royalty is born in exquisite settings, like palaces. The King of kings is born in straw surrounded by animals.

Perhaps their body heat helped reduce the cold climate.

Did Joseph find a mid-wife?

In Saint John's Gospel, he tells us that Jesus by his birth pitched his tent among us.

The Presentation

As obedient observers of the Mosaic Law, Joseph and Mary take their new-born, first-born Son, to the temple in Jerusalem to be consecrated to God and for Mary to be cleansed.

Saint Luke tells us that Joseph and Mary brought one of the sacrifices that was available to the poor: a pair of turtledoves or two young pigeons.[61]

---

[61] Luke 2:24

This trip to fulfill these two Jewish prescriptions was intended as a joyful occasion, and it was, but it turned to be a bittersweet situation when they meet Simeon and hear him prophesize about Jesus and Mary. The senior citizen Anna talks to everybody who will listen to her about the child Jesus!

The Finding of Jesus in the Temple

We go from the temple to the temple. We go from Jesus the newly born to Jesus the twelve-year-old.

We get caught up in a painful situation for Mary and Joseph. Their Son is missing for three days, and they have no idea where he is. Has he been kidnapped and sold into slavery? Has he been severely hurt? Has he run off in another caravan?

His parents find him in the temple, and Mary tells him in no uncertain terms:

> "Son, why have you treated us so? Behold, your father and I have been looking for you anxiously."[62]

And Jesus replies that he has been about his Father's business. Jesus' mission has begun. Was the twelve-year-old being insensitive and thoughtless to the most loving persons in existence? Is that even possible? But Mary is clear: "We are going home now!"

---

[62] Luke 2:48

The Sorrowful Mysteries

[A few thoughts of mine that you may find helpful.]

Where was Our Lady during the first three Sorrowful mysteries: the agony in the garden, the scourging at the pillar, the crowning with thorns?

My guess: Mary was in the upper room where they had celebrated the Last Supper.

After the Last Supper, Jesus and the Apostles had gone to the Garden of Gethsemane.

I have a suspicion that a young teenage disciple kept an eye on Gethsemane, and when the Romans came to arrest Jesus, the girl reported to Mother Mary what had transpired.

Mary knew that her Son would be mocked and suffer severe pain, which he had never experienced before, from the Roman military who treated him like play-toy.

When the soldiers brought Jesus out in public, Mary saw the crown of thorns and the blood dripping down his face and back. She saw the exposed flesh of her Son from the scourging at the pillar.

She knew that Jesus had had no sleep, no food, no drink; she knew that he was exhausted.

Now she watched as the soldiers paraded Jesus through the streets to scare the citizens of what might happen to them if they began to congregate or protest.

From a short distance, Mary watch the henchmen nail her Son's feet and hands to the rough wooden cross.

When Jesus was up-righted, along with the two criminals, the soldiers finished their work and returned to the barracks, except for a handful of men. Mary and Saint John, who had joined her, approached the cross, now the tree of life!

On the cross, before them, hung the naked body of Jesus struggling to breathe; they observed the body cramps inflicting intense pain; blood kept dripping out from various levels of his body. As he struggled to move himself into a position to breathe better, it was to no avail. Over the years, the Romans had mastered the technique of crucifixion; it was a horrifying way to die, ultimately by asphyxiation.

Mary and John struggled to hear Jesus' seven last words; his voice was so weak; he struggled to speak in-between the little breath he could muster.

Mary and John heard Jesus' gift:

"Woman, behold your son."
"Behold, your mother."[63]

She heard her Son speak to his Father:

"Father, into your hands, I commend mt spirit."[64]

The two watched as the soldier pierced Jesus' heart.[65]

Several came, one of whom specialized in removing the huge nails, more like spikes! They carefully took the limp body from the crossbeam and, at his Mother's insistence, laid him in her lap. She who knew him first before anyone in the world, who loved him first, who believed in him first; she now was first to hold his adult dead body.

Disciples came and took the body to the tomb for burial.

Joseph of Arimathea made arrangements with Pilate.[66]

---

[63] John 19: 27
[64] Luke 23:46
[65] John 19: 34
[66] John 19:38

The Glorious Mysteries

[A few thoughts of mine that you may find helpful.]

The Resurrection

I thank God the Father – Abba – for raising Jesus from the dead.

Jesus, the Son of God, and God the Father had such an intimate relationship during his earthy life of thirty-three years.

How often do we read in sacred scripture that Jesus would go off by himself to pray, to converse, with his Abba?

Jesus gives us such an inspiring example to cultivate a deep relationship with God the Father. Do we feel at ease in calling God Abba?

The Ascension

Jesus has completed his mission, the purpose for his incarnation.

Before he went back to heaven, he appeared to various people, at least eleven are specified in the New Testament. But there is one not mentioned that I must believe that he appeared to, before anyone else: his Mother Mary.

I remember spending a lot of time in mediation on this during the thirty-day retreat at Guelph, Ontario, Canada. Who was the first one who saw him at his birth? Who was the first to love him? Who was his first disciple? Who was with him to the last breath off his life on earth?

To whom would the Risen Jesus appear first? Mary![67]

This was the belief of Saint Ignatius Loyola; this was the belief of Pope Saint John Paul II. This is my belief also.[68]

The Descent of the Holy Spirit

The Holy Spirit, The Spirit of Truth, The Spirit of Love, the one who overshadowed Mary.

The Holy Spirit came upon the disciples and Mary in the Upper Room.[69]

It is Pentecost, the birthday of the Church![70]

We pray and ask the Holy Spirit to come upon us, to enlighten our minds, to encourage our wills.

We need to be courageous Christians today! To be bold Catholics!

> "Come, Holy Spirit, fill the hearts of your faithful and enkindle in us the fire of your love!"

We said this prayer to the Holy Spirit before all our classes, talks, etc. in the seminary. It was one that Saint Vincent de Paul usually used before his presentations. I use the prayer often before my talks.

---

[67] The Spiritual Exercises, The Fourth Week
[68] General Audience, May 21, 1997
[69] Acts 1:14
[70] Acts 2:4

The Assumption

The Eastern Rite Catholics call this event, this feast: The Dormition: Mary fell asleep, and when she woke up, who is standing there? The glorified Risen Jesus.

And she, body and soul, is there in this new dimension of existence that we really do not know much about. We can speculate, but that is all.

You and I will one day, God willing, fall asleep and wake up in this new dimension. We will face Judge Jesus.

And after Jesus' Second Coming, we will be wherever we will be, body and soul.

The Coronation

Our Lady is crowned Queen of Heaven and Earth. The Queen of queens, The Lady of ladies.

Who is she next to? The King of kings and The Lord of lords.

Mary is Queen Mother. If Jesus is King, and he is, she who gave birth to him, must, therefore, be Queen Mother.

What do we pray at the end of the Rosary?

"Hail, Holy Queen…"

The Luminous Mysteries

[A few thoughts of mine that you may find helpful.]

We are creatures of habit. For years, I prayed the three sets of mysteries of the Rosary: Joyful, Glorious, and Sorrowful. Then in October 2002, Pope Saint John Paul II introduced the Church to "The Mysteries of Light" or, as many call them, "The Luminous Mysteries."

The Baptism of Jesus

Jesus leaves Nazareth and travels to Jerusalem. When he arrives, John the Baptism is performing a water ceremony as symbolic of a person's change to lead a better life. It is not the sacrament of baptism. Jesus's acceptance of John's ritual is a means of identifying with the rest of humankind; it has nothing to do with his divinity.

Jesus has left his "hidden life" after thirty years and begins living his public life. A drastic change of lifestyle including the departure from the trade of carpentry.

What do we hear and see? The confirmation of the Father and the Holy Spirit: Jesus is divine!

"This is my beloved Son, with whom I am well pleased."[71]

The Heavenly Father is explicit: "*My* Son in whom I am well pleased."

---

[71] Matthew 3: 17

Jesus is the missionary of the Father. The Holy Trinity stamps their approval for Jesus' public ministry. He now begins to teach and preach God's plan—God's will for all of us.

The Wedding at Cana

There is a wedding and Jesus' Mother has been invited; Jesus attends with several of his new disciples.

Mary notices that the wine is running out; the married couple surely will be embarrassed. She cannot do anything about it, but she knows who can.

In obedience to his Mother, Jesus does do something. How can he refuse a request of love?

Mother Mary tells the servants to be obedient: "Do whatever he tells you." And they do.

There is a beautiful stained-glass window in Saint Vincent's Church, Chicago where I was pastor. The window displays the water being poured into the wine jar, and as the water is being poured, the color white changes to red; the miracle was happening as the servants were pouring!

The Proclamation of the Kingdom

I have heard that the foundation of all of Jesus' teaching, preaching, and actions can be summarized in one sentence, and that sentence is found in the Gospel of Saint Mark:

> "The time is fulfilled, and the kingdom of God has come near: repent and believe in the good news."[72]

---

[72] Mark 1:15

I sometimes say: "I'm going to chapel to pray for my conversion."
Is there any one time when any of us are completely converted?

How many times have I prayed: "Thy kingdom come, thy will be done…"?

The Catechism of the Catholic Church reminds us that everyone is called to enter the kingdom.[73] This includes the good guys and bad guys and everyone in-between.

Pope Saint John Paul II said in his apostolic letter on the Rosary:

> "Each of these mysteries is a revelation of the Kingdom now present in the very person of Jesus."[74]

The Transfiguration

I have had the blessing of being on Mount Tabor on two trips to the Holy Land.

The last time it was late and getting dark; the Franciscans were locking up. Out in the valley at a distance, a thunderstorm was brewing.

Jesus took his inner circle up the mountain (Peter, James, and John).[75] It had to be a good hike up to the top for the four of them. Each time we took a car.

Jesus displayed his divinity. His face is like the sun; his garments became white as light; Moses and Elijah appear. Those things alone would prove his divinity, but there was more: they hear the Father's voice (somewhat a duplication of what was heard at Jesus' baptism with additional words): "This is my beloved Son, with whom I am well pleased; listen to him."

---

[73] CCC # 543
[74] On the Most Holy Rosary, Pope John Paul II, # 21
[75] Matthew 17:1

The Father says to you and me: "Listen to him." And what does Our Lady say?

"Do whatever he tells you." The key to holiness of life: "Do God's will."

The word "obedience" in Latin means "to listen."

The Institution of the Eucharist

I am blessed daily to receive the Body and Blood of Our Lord and Savior Jesus Christ. Even during these months of lockdown because of the virus, our community has had the celebration of the Eucharist daily.

I need spiritual food for my spiritual life. The difference: I do not change Jesus into me; he changes me into him.

I pray that I may acquire a deeper love for the Holy Eucharist. Focusing on the meaning of the words of Jesus used at the Last Supper, may my hope come true.

Many years ago, when I was a deacon, my professor in sacred scripture asked me to write a paper on the words of consecration at Mass. I have never forgotten that time. In the language Jesus spoke, Aramaic, his words meant "This bread and wine are my whole self."

Queen Mother

"A great sign appeared in heaven, a woman clothed with the sun, with the moon under her feet, and on her head a crown of twelve stars; she was with child…
she brought forth a male child, one who is to rule all the nations with a rod of iron, but her child was caught up to God and to his throne…"[76]

In how many apparitions in this book alone have we read of Mary wearing a crown of twelve stars? Mary is queen; she is Queen Mother in every apparition whether she is wearing her crown or not. As she appears to her children, she is Queen of Heaven and Earth to give them advice, inspiration, and hope.

If Jesus is King of kings and Lord of lords as sacred scripture says.[77] Then the woman who gave birth to him must be Queen Mother.

What do we pray in the fifth Glorious Mystery: The Coronation of Mary, the crowning of Mary Queen of Heaven? We pray this mystery every Wednesday and Sunday, which means that the ordinary Catholic who prays the Rosary thinks about Queen Mary a good deal!

Mary is Queen Mother of Heaven and Earth. As Saint John Damascene wrote:

---

[76] The Book of Revelation 12:1-2, 5
[77] Revelation 19:16

"When she became mother of the creator, she truly became queen of every creature."[78]

When I meditate on this Glorious Mystery, I usually think of Mary as Queen of queens, Lady of ladies…as compared to her Son, the Kings of kings, the Lord of lords. I would be curious to know of your reflections.

The Queen Mother sits on a throne next to the King of Heaven and Earth.

[78] Ad Caeli Reginam, Pope Pius XII, #34

The Subversive Song of Mary

Did you know that? Did you know that the Song of Mary, the Magnificat,[79] was banned by a few governments?

+ During the British Rule in India, the singing of the Magnificat in church was prohibited because of its inflammable words. On the final day of British rule, Gandhi, a non-Christian, requested Mary's song be read in all places where the British flag was being lowered.
+ The government of Guatemala during the 1980's saw the ideas raised by Our Lady's song of God's special concern for the poor dangerous and revolutionary; it banned any public recitation of Mary's words.
+ The dictatorship in Argentina banned Mary's song after the "Mothers of the Disappeared" displayed its words on placards in the capital plaza.

The German Lutheran theologian Dietrich Bonhoeffer in a sermon during Advent on December 17, 1933 said:

"The song of Mary...is at once the most passionate, the wildest...the most revolutionary Advent hymn every sung. This is not the gentle, tender, dreamy Mary whom we sometimes see in paintings...This

---

[79] Luke 1:46-55

96

song has none of the sweet, nostalgic, or even playful tones of some of the Christmas cards."

Were these people serious? Did they truly see Our Lady's Song, her Magnificat, subversive, revolutionary? Yes, they did. These governments did not want the poor and needy to get any ideas about protests or more!

But we say: I pray Mary's Song every day and I never get any ideas that those leaders got.

May I make a suggestion? Sometime soon when you pray her Song, try to uncover what Mary meant by her words. What did she expect, what did she see, what did she anticipate?

Allow me to give you one of my takes on Mary's Song.[80]

It is a song of HOPE. It is the song of the people of God walking through history. It is the song of many saints, of our own forefathers and foremothers who have walked in faith before us. It is the song of those who have faced the struggles of life while carrying in their heart the hope of the humble ones like Our Lady Mary.

"My soul glorifies the Lord." This song is sung throughout world.

In those countries where the church is greatly suffering, this song is strong.

Where the cross is, there is hope always. If there is no hope, we are not Christians.

My friends, do not be robbed of hope because this is a grace, a gift of God which carries us forward, onward with our eyes fixed on eternal life, eternal happiness.

We sing with Mary. We sing her song of hope.

---

[80] Read Pope Francis' homily on the Feast of the Assumption, August 15, 2013

Sub Tuum

Here is a question: what is the oldest known prayer to the Blessed Virgin Mary? This sounds like a trivial pursuit question. It is not meant to be. Most would say "The Hail Mary" but that would be incorrect.

During the horrific persecution led by the Roman Emperor Decius in 250 A.D. against Christianity, the monks in Egypt popularized a hymn to Our Lady begging for her protection. The prayer originally was composed in Greek,[81] but we know it in its Latin and English translations.

> An English translation from the Greek:
> "Beneath your compassion,
> we take refuge, O Mother of God ("Theotokos")
> do not despise our petitions in time of trouble:
> but rescue us from dangers,
> only pure, only blessed one."

You who recite the Divine Office are familiar with "Sub Tuum" used as the antiphon for the Nunc Dimittis at Compline in the Little Office of the Blessed Virgin Mary; in the Liturgy of the Hours it may be used as the Marian antiphon after Compline outside of Eastertide.

Pope Francis asked to pray Sub Tuum along with the Rosary and the Prayer to Saint Michael asking for unity of the Church during

---

[81] John Rylands papyrus 470, in a collection at the University of Manchester.

October (2018) in the face of scandals and accusations. Although the Pope's request was a few years ago, it is still relevant; it can still be beneficial for the Church at large and for our own personal spiritual life.

We have seen open persecution of ancient communities of the faithful over recent years, especially in the lands which first received the Gospel itself. People are killed, churches bombed and burned, believers prevented from divine worship, all because they profess Christianity.

We need to pray for these Christians. Things are getting bad here in the United States; God is disappearing in thought, word, and deed, and there is greater secularization than ever, and it is not over.

If "Sub Tuum" was seen as a beneficial prayer to Mary during times of persecution, is it not a good one for today?

> We fly to your protection, O holy Mother of God.
> despise not our petitions in our necessities,
> but deliver us always from all dangers,
> O glorious and Blessed Virgin. Amen.

Little Lady Dressed in Blue

My aunt Lill Hall taught me my first prayers. She and Uncle Bill lived with us; things were tough economically at that time in our country, and we were one extended family in our apartment above a store on North Avenue, east of Crawford (Pulaski) in Chicago.

When I ready for bed, Aunt Lill would come, and we would say prayers together. Even though I was three years old, I have vivid memories of this.

Lill taught me: "Little Lady Dressed in Blue."[82]

That first verse asks Mother Mary:

> "Teach me how to pray!
> God was just your little boy,
> Tell me what to say!
>
> Did you hold his hand at night?
> Did you ever try
> Telling stories of the world?
> O! And did he cry?
>
> Lovely Lady dressed in blue…"

---

[82] The author is Mary Dixon Thayer who wrote more than one poem for Our Lady. This poem was written in 1926.

When Our Lady looked at her little Son, she knew that he was flesh and blood, and he would suffer. And, as Simeon told her in the temple, her heart a sword shall pierce.

She had no idea how her Son would suffer. She found out.

Little Lady dressed in blue, who suffers the most?

12 Stars

I have quoted the Book of Revelation a few times already in the text, particularly Chapter 12:1. I present it again because it is apropos.

> "And a great sign appeared in heaven, a woman
> clothed with the sun, with the moon under her feet,
> and on her head a crown of twelve stars."

A crown of 12 stars. In apparition after apparition as we will see in the next section of the book, Mary appeared often wearing a crown of twelve stars.

What is the meaning of the crown and its number?

It seems to be the common opinion of all authors that the twelve stars on Our Lady's crown represents the twelve patriarchs of the tribes of Israel (the original people of God) and the twelve apostles (the renewed people of God).

I learned something else about Mary's crown that I had not known before when I read an article by Father Johann Rotten, S.M.[83]

The article is entitled "The Meaning of the Twelve Stars of Revelation" in which Father Rotten presents the twelve stars as referring to the graces, privileges, and charisms received by Our Lady.

Our Blessed Lady is crowned with her perfections, one star for each of the perfections.

---

[83] Meaning of the Twelve Stars of Revelation, Johann Rotten, S.M., University of Dayton. I cannot recommend the University of Dayton enough to you. They have excellent materials on the Blessed Virgin Mary.

Here is the appropriate list of the perfections.[84]

1. Predestination before creation
2. Conceived without original sin
3. Overshadowed by the Holy Spirit
4. Virgin before, during, and after giving birth to Jesus
5. Theotokos (God-giver) of Jesus
6. Fullness of grace (kecharitomena)
7. Introduced to the mystery of the Holy Trinity
8. Seat of Wisdom
9. Superior to angels and humans
10. Coronation of Queen of Heaven and Earth
11. Called to be Mediatrix
12. Revered by all creatures

---

[84] I have made a few changes for clarification purposes.

The Hands of Mary

Growing up, our family did not have the appliances which are expected in today's households. I am referring to a refrigerator, washer and dryer, garbage disposal, dishwasher.

My mother's hands were calloused, rough, knuckles sometimes swollen, nails short and skin occasionally cracked with slight bleeding. In our first home, she shoveled coal into our one stove in the middle of the basement flat and cleaned out ashes when needed. In the first and second houses her hands did not improve: she did the dishes in the kitchen sink's hot water, did the family laundry in a large sink, mopped the kitchen floor's linoleum, cleaned out the icebox and ice-compartment above, etc.

I doubt if she ever had a manicure let alone a pedicure. I do not remember her using a potion for her hands. One reason: she used the money for the family needs rather than for herself.

What about Mary's hands? She had to sweep the dirt floor of the house and wipe off the table and chairs with hot water. Our Lady had to do a load of laundry outside on the rocks; she had to fetch water from the neighboring well for cooking and cleaning. Carrying heavy buckets, using heated water for the clothing, cleaning, cooking all took their toll on her hands.

I must think that Mary's hands were much like my mother's: calloused, tough-skinned, cracked, sometimes swollen from constant use.

After her Assumption into heaven, it was a difficult story: her hands became smooth and soft. We see this in her apparitions.

What about our hands? Do they get dirty from doing random acts of charity?

Marian Apparitions

Our Lady of the Pillar

I am beginning this section of the book on Marian Apparitions with what tradition tells us is the very first apparition of Blessed Mary while she was still alive. Many appearances of Our Lady fascinate me; this one, Our Lady of Pillar, has fascinated me like no other. Why? For many reasons which will enfold as you read and hopefully reflect on the material.

I never knew about Our Lady of the Pillar until I heard our Vincentian seminarians from Spain talk about her. I was blessed to have five Spanish Vincentian seminarians ordained to the priesthood with me. They all knew about this Marian devotion so popular in their homeland.

Fast forward: when I worked at the National Office of the Society of Saint Vincent de Paul in Saint Louis, I drove down Lindbergh Blvd past Our Lady of the Pillar Church staffed by the Marianists. One of the priests in the parish was my spiritual director and confessor.

****

Why begin this section of the book with Our lady of Pillar from Spain? As I mentioned, because it was the first Marian apparition in history: Mary appeared to Saint James the Great, brother of Saint John. Why? Because it necessitated bilocation on Mary's part as she was living in Ephesus and James was in Zaragoza, Spain, by land, 2457 miles away.

One night as James was praying, somewhat discouraged by his setbacks at evangelization with the local citizenry, out of nowhere, a great light engulfed him. James fell to the ground, staring at the brilliant light. Out of the light appeared the Blessed Virgin whom he personally knew from Jerusalem. She was surrounded by countless angels.

From my best calculations, Mary must have been 54 years old. She appeared to James at the Ebro River on October 12, 40 AD, seven years after Jesus died and rose from the dead.

Bilocation: did Mary bilocate? She had to. In later times, we have substantiated, for example, the bilocation of Saint Martin Porres, O.P. and Saint Padre Pio, Capuchin. Other saints did it.

Remember, we are talking about the Mother of God here. We are talking about God power. Nothing is impossible with God. And we are talking about James, an apostle of Jesus. If the Risen Savior wanted to encourage James to persevere in his efforts of evangelization and considered that his Mother would be the best way to do this, he sent her. Bilocation was a means to an end. In my mind, it is that simple.

Did she appear as 54 years old or younger? From my research on apparitions, Mary appears in various heights and ages.

Mary appeared to Saint James standing on a column, a pillar, of jasper. Jasper is commonly red in color; we have no idea of what color this pillar was.

Mary gave James a statue of herself holding the Child Jesus. From the description that we have received, Mary appeared as a young mother holding Jesus as an infant, who was, in fact, in the year of 40 AD, an adult resurrected seven years earlier.

In all apparitions, when she appears holding the Child Jesus, Mary comes as the Mother of Jesus, the Mother of God. For example, in 1830, Mary appeared to St. Catherine Laboure, the Daughter of Charity of St. Vincent de Paul, as a young woman but without the child. Mary came charged with a mission to Catherine. You will read similarities in other Marian appearances in this section of the book.

Mary standing on the pillar with the Child Jesus asked that a chapel be built on the site of the apparition. Her promise:

> "that God may work miracles and wonders through
> my intercession for all those who place themselves
> under my patronage."

Saint James with his disciples did as directed. The Church of Our Lady of the Pillar in Zaragoza is the first church dedicated to Mary in history.

Saint James returned to Jerusalem from Spain. In the year 44 AD, he was beheaded. The disciples took his body back to Spain for final burial. The statue and pillar given by the Blessed Mother were retained by the faithful of Zaragoza.

The original statue was destroyed in the 1434 fire. The present statue dates from the mid-fifteenth century.

Many miracles testify to the statue of Our Lady and its origin. For example, in 1936, during the Spanish Civil War, one of the political groups bombed the shrine, but the bombs that hit the church never exploded.

The most well-known miracle occurred in the 17th century, when a beggar, Miguel Pellicer, who was unable to work due to an amputated leg, had his leg restored while praying at the shrine.

Presently, four priests assigned to oversee the statue are the only ones who can touch the statue except newborn infants who are lifted to touch the statue.

Down through the centuries, popes have encouraged pilgrimages to the shrine of Our Lady of Pillar. The authenticity of the shrine was approved under Pope Callistus III who issued a bull on September 23, 1456, giving a seven-year indulgence for those who visit the shrine. The feast day was officially introduced in 1640.

Innocent III, on August 7, 1723, approved the apparition as canonical. In 1730, Pope Clement allowed the feast of Our Lady of the Pillar to be celebrated throughout the Spanish Empire.

Over the years, I wonder how many girls I had baptized and married with the name of "Maria del Pilar." It has been a popular name for Hispanic girls. Our Lady of Pillar also holds a special place in the history and mission of several religious organizations, e.g., the Marianists and Opus Dei.

Our Lady of the Pillar's feast day is October 12th.

Our Lady of Sorrows

At the cross, her station keeping,
Stood the mournful Mother weeping,
Close to Jesus to the last.[85]

Many of us know this sequence from Lent or from praying the Stations of the Cross or from the Mass in honor of Our Lady of Sorrows, September 15th.

It is a haunting first verse, the melody as well as the words.

Mary at the foot of the cross happened two thousand years ago, but it is still happening today.

Almost daily we open a magazine or a newspaper or see on our computer a picture of a mother holding her child shot or killed by a stray bullet on our city streets.

That is a mother of sorrows.

What about those indigenous mothers whose children are among the "disappeared"? Those are mothers of sorrows.

Whenever we see a dead child, son, or daughter, in the arms of its mother, we ask ourselves, who has suffered more?

That is why we honor Mother Mary, Mother of Sorrows, who had such an intimate sharing in the suffering of the person of her only Son, Jesus.

Mary who waited near the cross while her naked Son was

---

[85] Stabat Mater Dolorosa attributed to Brother Jacopone da Todi, OFM (1230-1306) but the latest research says the sequence (poem) may have been an earlier work of the Dominican nuns in Bologna (13th century)

experiencing horrific body spasms and asphyxiation. When he had breathed his last, she waited "close to Jesus to the last." It had to be heart-wrenching to see them removing the blunt nails from his hands and feet.

Michelangelo captured this extreme suffering in the Pieta. We see the dead limp Jesus draped over in the lap of his Mother. She is the Lady of Sorrows from the foot of the cross to the taking down of his body to his entombment.

Mary knows suffering. She is ever ready to hear us in our sorrows and agony.

Some churches have an image of the Virgin of Sorrows. Often, she is dressed in black lace, sometimes holding Jesus' crown of thorns, sometimes has one or seven swords piercing her silver heart.[86] At times, the Virgin of Sorrows is standing alone or as part of a "Calvario" with Saint John as they flank the crucified Jesus.[87]

Devotion to our Sorrowful Mother is a source of comfort and pillar of hope. She is our refuge and our strength.

---

[86] Luke 2:35
[87] John 19:26-27

Our Lady of La Salette

The apparition of Our Lady of La Salette sounds like that of Our Lady of Sorrows, except at La Salette, she appeared in the French Alps at the southeastern part of France close to Switzerland at 5,705 feet.

It was close to 3 pm Saturday, September 19, 1846. Two youngsters, Melanie Mathieu, age 14, and Maximin Giraud, age 11, while tending cows, decided to take a nap in the field. When they awoke, they saw that their cows had strayed. Searching for them, they were attracted by a brilliant light and, as they crossed a dried-up creek, they saw a beautiful lady with her head in her hands. She was crying her eyes out.

Her headdress shone with a diadem of rays and of roses. A white shawl was thrown over her shoulders and crossed around the waist, bordered with a garland of roses. The dress of light was pure white and flecked with specks of gold. On her chest, inside, was a crucifix, with a hammer and nails. To support the cross and the body of Christ, there was a little chain round the neck; then a second chain, like a braid but without rings, seemed to crush the shoulders beneath it by its great weight, as though to symbolize the burden of our sins. Finally, there was a golden yellow apron and white shoes with a golden buckle and a cluster of roses,[88]

The Lady told them

> "Come, my children, do not be afraid: I am here to proclaim great news to you."

---

[88] See "The Secret of La Sallette" by Father Giray, Missionary of La Sallete, 1911

The Lady began to speak first in French, then in patois. (These children were not very educated) What followed was "a mother's correction" of her children at large. She spoke in prophetic terms to make people see that reconciliation was desirable and achievable. [89]

Her remarks were a mixture of complaints, reproaches, warnings, and threats. Our Lady called a spade a spade; she was blatantly honest.

Our Lady deplored the practices of those who blaspheme, profane Sunday, violate the law of abstinence, no longer pray, seldom attend Mass, provoke the divine wrath, and weight down the avenging arm of her Son ready to strike, and exposing themselves to every kind of scourge, private and public.

That was quite a bit for those kids to grasp!

"If My people are not willing to submit themselves, I am forced to let go of my Son's arm…For all this time I have suffered for you! If I do not wish my Son to abandon you, I must take it upon myself to pray for this continually….In vain will you pray, in vain will you act, you will never be able to make up for the trouble I have taken for you al!

"I kept the seventh (day) for myself and no one wishes to grant me that one day…

Those who drive carts cannot swear without adding my Son's name. These are two things which weigh down the arm of my Son so much.

"If the harvest is spoiled, it is only because of you others. I made you see this last year with the potatoes….it was quite the opposite when you found bad potatoes; you swore oaths, and you included the

---

[89] See "La Salette – Questions and Answers, Fr. Normand Theroux, M.S.

name of my Son. They will continue to go bad; at Christmas there will be none left."

"If you have corn, you must not sow it. The beasts will eat all that you sow,

And all that grows will fall to dust when you thresh it. A great famine will come. Before the famine comes, children under the age of seven will begin to tremble and will die in the arms of those who hold them. The others will do penance through hunger. The nuts will go bad, the grapes will become rotten."

Our Lady asked the two:

"Do you say your prayers properly?"

They replied: "No, Madame, not so much."

"Ah, my children, you must say them morning and evening, when you can do no more, say a Pater and an Ave Maria; and when you have the time to do better, you will say more."

"Only a few old women go to Mass; in the summer, the rest work all day and, in the winter, when they do not know what to do, they only go Mass to make fun of religion. During Lent, they go to the butcher's like hungry dogs!"

Mary spoke of spoiled wheat. "I don't know who will be eating anything next year if the wheat is spoiled….".
The Blessed Virgin ended her words:

"And so, my children, you will pass this on to all my people."

And without looking back, she repeated those words to the children as she crossed the stream. She rose from the ground to regain the heights of heaven.

Maximin and Melanie hurried with their flock to the village to tell the masters all that they had seen and heard on the mountain.

Some personal observations:

One of the commonalities of all apparitions heard from all visionaries: Our Lady adopts her dress to that of the area but with better accessories, and she is beautiful.

Mary is sitting down the whole time of the apparition and she is crying; tears rolling down her beautiful face. This is rare.

She talks to a girl 14 and a boy 11 who had met only a few days before.

The two children were not well educated. Mary had to switch languages.

Did Our Lady select the two because of their simplicity and humility?

Our Blessed Mother gave a secret to both but neither knew the other's secret, and both never revealed it their entire life.

Our Lady only appeared one time at La Salette.

Mary is quite strong in her criticism of the people.

La Salette is not an easy place to get to for pilgrims; those with cardiac or pulmonary conditions would find it difficult because of the high attitude.

Our Lady's predictions about the crops came true.

The two children saw Mary ascend into heaven which is also rare.

A community of priests and brothers was founded by the Bishop of Grenoble, France in 1852: "The Missionaries of La Salette."

The apparitions were approved by the Church in 1851.

"Let us meet at the foot of the cross,
where we will find strength and courage."
(Saint Bernadette Soubirous)

Our Lady of Guadalupe

I discovered Our Lady of Guadalupe some sixty-plus years ago at my first assignment as a priest at Saint Vincent de Paul Church, Pampa, Texas. The Mexican ladies were interested in starting a "sociedad" called "Las Guadalupanas." So, I contacted the office then in San Antonio, Texas, and we were on our way.

The ladies wanted a statue of Our Lady of Guadalupe; I agreed. Once a month, they made tamales from scratch. With the money earned, I bought a beautiful carved plaque of Our Lady from Italy. It hangs today on the wall of the Church of Saint Vincent de Paul in Pampa, Texas.

Incidentally, those tamales were the best I ever had in my life!

****

In 1531, on the hill called Tepeyac then outside Mexico City, the Virgin Mary introduced herself to the world as its Mother and, in fact, the Mother of Humanity under the title that we know: The Virgin of Guadalupe.

An Indian peasant, Juan Diego, saw a gleaning light on Tepeyac and heard a woman's voice calling him. He climbed the hill and there before him was a woman who identified herself as the Virgin Mary. She told Juan that she wanted a sanctuary build there on the spot for her to show and share her love, compassion, and protection with her devoted children.

Juan visited the Archbishop, Juan de Zumarraga, but he did not believe Juan. He told the man that he needed proof beyond the shadow of a doubt, conclusive proof, of the story and of the Lady's identity.

The next day, Juan's uncle was seriously ill, and Juan went to get a priest to give uncle the last rites. Juan tried to shirt past the hill, but Our Lady met him and told him that his uncle was already cured.

Juan relayed to Our Lady what he had experienced with the archbishop. She told Juan to pick some of flowers that he saw. Although it was December, the cold of winter, and nothing should have been in bloom, Juan picked gorgeous flowers he had never seen before. The Virgin bundled the flowers into Juan's tilma.

When Juan returned to the office of the archbishop, and he presented his tilma of the flowers, the archbishop recognized them as Castilian Roses which do not grow in Mexico.

But more significantly was the miraculous imprint on the tilma: the colorful icon of the Virgin herself. Her icon was precisely how Juan had described her.

As the roses fell to the floor, the archbishop fell to his knees.

When Juan returned home, his uncle was indeed completely cured. In his own language, his uncle told those present that the Virgin Mary called herself what sounded like Guadalupe, the famous shrine in Spain.

The archbishop ordered a church to be constructed as Our Lady had requested and the tilma with its icon was enshrined. Later, in 1976, a basilica was built and the famous tilma was encased there.

****

I have been blessed to have venerated in both the ancient church and new basilica in Mexico City. It is inspiring to see people from various levels of society doing penance by crawling on their knees across the huge plaza to the basilica.

These are people of faith, hope, and charity.

****

In 1945, the year that World War II had ended, Pope Pius XII declared Our Lady of Guadalupe patroness of the Americas.

Our Lady said to Juan Diego:

> "I am your Compassionate Mother. Yours, for you yourself, for everybody here in the land, for each and all together, for all others too, for all folk of every kind...here I shall listen to their groanings, to their saddening here shall I make well and heal up their each and every kind of disappointment of exhausting pangs, of bitter pain."

Not only is Our Lady of Guadalupe one of the earliest Marian apparitions, but it is also the only time that Our Lady has gifted us with her portrait.

Eight years after the apparition, eight million people embraced the Catholic faith in the New World.

Saint Pope John Paul II, who visited the Shrine of Our Lady in 1979, described the Guadalupe as

> "The beginning of evangelization with a vitality that surpassed all expectations, Christ's message through his Mother took up the central elements of the indigenous culture, purified them, and gave them the definitive sense of salvation."

Our Lady of Guadalupe and Juan Diego were missionaries par excellence!

The Blessed Mother chose an indigenous person, a common man, probably illiterate, to appear to. That is a classic empowerment!

Our Lady of Guadalupe is affectionately called "La Virgen Morenita" because of the color of her face.

The Pro-Life movement has adapted Our Lady of Guadalupe as

their patroness because her belt is interpreted as a sign of pregnancy. Our Lady came to Mexico in 1531 as a young pregnant girl carrying the baby Jesus within her womb.

Our Lady turned the Aztecs from a worldview of despair to one of hope!

Our Lady of Akita (Japan)

Our Lady of Akita is a newer apparition for me. I only came to know anything about this after I moved into my current residence. On our property (which I have mentioned elsewhere in this text) there is a Marian Meditation Walk. In this "ring," this circle of Mary, is the statue of Our Lady of Akita.

I find this apparition of Mary to be most unusual. I do not know of any appearance like it. Yes, I am aware that each apparition is special for the occasion, location, and person/s involved but, as you will see, these apparitions to Sister Agnes are quite unique and, not to be disrespectful, weird.

A few general statements:

+ Our Lady of Akita is the Virgin Mary associated with a wooden statue venerated by faithful Japanese who believe it to be miraculous.
+ The image of Mary is the one known due to apparitions reported in 1973 by Sister Agnes Katsuko Sasagawa in the outskirt of Akita, Japan.
+ The messages emphasize prayer, especially saying the Rosary, and penance, prophesying persecution of priests and heresy in the Catholic Church.
+ The apparitions of the weeping statue of Mary was broadcast on Japanese national television and gained further attention

with the sudden healing of the hearing impairment experienced by Sister Agnes Sasagawa after the apparitions.

+ Bishop John Shojiro Ito of Niigata authorized the veneration of the Holy Mother of Akita in his 1984 pastoral letter.

In 1973, Sr. Agnes reported apparitions, as well as stigmata and a wooden statue of Mary which was said to have wept on 101 occasions. The nuns at the house reported the stigmata on the statue as well as on the hands of Sister Agnes. According to the Sisters, the stigmata appeared before the tears started and ended after the tears. The blood type of the statue and its sweat and tear type were found to be types B and AB, respectively.

Sr. Agnes reported three messages from the Blessed Virgin during 1973; the statue itself continued weeping. Sister first heard the statue calling her and then the first message began.

1. The first message of Mary (July 6, 1973): the statue became illuminated as it acknowledged Sister Agnes' stigmata and hearing impairment. She was to recite the prayer of the Handmaids of the Eucharist which the Virgin Mary said would cure her deafness. Mary asked for the praying of the Rosary and Acts of Reparation.

2. In the second message Our Lady says:
    "Many men in this world afflict the Lord. I desire souls to console him to soften the anger of the Heavenly Father. I wish, with my Son, for souls who will repair by their suffering and their poverty for the sinners and ingrates,"

3. In the third message of October 13, 1973, the statue became animated for a time as witnessed by a few nuns.

"My dear daughter, listen well to what I have to say.

...if men do not repent and better themselves, the Father will inflict a terrible punishment on all humanity...greater than the deluge, as never seen before.

Fire will fall from the sky and wipe out a great part of humanity...good as well as bad, sparing neither priests nor faithful. The survivors will find themselves so desolate that they will envy the dead. Each day recite the prayer of the Rosary...pray for the pope, bishops, priests...the devil will infiltrate even the Church ...cardinals opposing cardinals, bishops against other bishops.

Priests who venerate me will be scorned and opposed by their confreres...churches and altars sacked, the Church will be full of those who accept compromises and the demon will press many priests and consecrated souls to leave the service of the Lord. The demon will be especially implacable against souls consecrated to God.

The thought of the loss of so many souls is the cause of my sadness.

If sins increase in number and gravity, there will be no longer pardon for them.

With courage, speak to your superior....Today is the last time that I will speak to you in living voice. From now on you will obey the one sent to you and your superior...I alone am able to save you from the calamities which approach."

A Korean woman with a terminal brain tumor was miraculously

cured after friends and others prayed for the intercession of Our Lady of Akita. She received two visions of Mary during her recovery, the first while comatose. The cure was verified by medical professionals and declared miraculous by Church authorities of Korea. The date was August 4, 1981.

My comments: In Marian apparitions, no two are alike. Mary never appears in the same way: dress, complexion, language, posture, etc. Often her message for the church at large is identical, but words to the visionaries are particularly appropriate.

> A question for reflection, considering Akita: which is easier for the Blessed Virgin: to appear physically or to make herself present through an object, e.g., wooden, plaster, etc.?

Our Lady of Fourviere

You may not know this shrine of Notre-Dame, but the Lyonnaise do!

She overlooks the great city of Lyon, France, as a mother watches over children.

I have had the privilege of praying at Fourviere several times. It has a great history.

The citizens of Lyon, the Lyonnaise, call it "the praying hill." I have a small but beautiful holy card from Fourviere with which I pray daily.

The early Christians expressed their faith in Fourviere. Saint Pothinus, the first Bishop of Lyon and first Bishop of Gaul, was martyred there as many others. The faithful placed themselves under the protection of Mary from the beginning.

In 1192, a church was built on the top of the hill in honor of the Virgin Mary and Saint Thomas of Canterbury. Ruined during the religious wars, the chapel was rebuilt in 1586.

Remember: the church on the hill looks down at the sprawling city of Lyon. Through the prayers and vows made to Mary, a special bond between the Lyonnaise and Fourviere was created over the years.

This is what I mean:

> In 1638, a serious epidemic of scurvy affected the children in the city; no available medication, nothing seemed able to stop it. People decided to go

in procession up the hill to Fourviere. The sickness gradually disappeared, never to return.

In 1643, a plague was devastating Europe. The aldermen promised to go to Fourviere, to offer a crown and a votive candle every year if their city of Lyon was shared. The tradition continues September 8, the Birthday of Mary, every year.

In 1832, cholera was hitting areas and threatening Lyon. The archbishop mandated public prayers. Once more, the Lyonnaise were spared. They thanked the Virgin Mary by painting a huge painting that hangs at the back of the Basilica today. The painting is the "tabeau d'Orsel."

In 1852, the bell of the Chapel of Our Lady was crowned by a statue made in golden bronze to thank God for her motherly protection. Bad weather postponed the inauguration because of the floods, but when the weather became calmer, the Lyonnaise lighted up the city spontaneously by placing lanterns on their windowsills.

They did the same thing two years later for the dogma of the Immaculate Conception proclamation. To this day, on December 8th, a procession from Saint John's Cathedral to Fourviere takes place. Catholics light up their windows with candles. Now, the city annually has been organizing the event "fete des lumieres" (feast of lights) which attracts millions of people.

In 1870, the Prussians were advancing toward the city. The Lyonnaise promised to erect a big church dedicated to Our Lady if their Lyon was spared. It was. Construction began two years later in 1872, consecrated on June 16, 1896, and declared a basilica on March 16, 1897.

****

One of the amazing things about Our Lady of Fourviere is the number of saints and remarkable men and women who have prayed at Our Lady's shrine.

+ Saint Therese Couderic who founded the Cenacle Sisters
+ Saint Claudine Thevenet, founder of Congregation of Sisters of Jesus and Mary
+ Mrs. Jeanne Carnier who initiated the chairable organization called "Oeuvre du Calvaire" (Incidentally, the first ones to use the word "hospice" to care for the dying)
+ Fathers Jean-laude Collin and Marcellin Champagnot who founded the Society of Mary (Marists) and the Little Brothers of Mary
+ Bishop Melchior de Marion Bresillac who started the Society of African Missions
+ Father Andre Coindee who founded the Brothers of the Sacred Heart
+ Father Louis Querbes who started the Clerics of Saint Viator
+ Saint Peter Julian Eymard who founded the Congregation of the Blessed Sacrament for men and one for women
+ Mr. Antoine-Frederic Ozanam who was the principal founder of the Society of Saint Vincent de Paul

Quite an impressive list who graced the pews of the Shrine of Our Lady of Fourviere!

The Blessed Mother's shrine in Lyon drew people to prayer and to allow Our Lady to exercises her Mother's love for the people in dire need as we saw in the serious epidemics and the threat of warfare.

The faith of the Lyonnaise, yesterday and today, allow Our Lady of Fourviere to be a refuge and a beacon of hope shining from the praying hill down into the expansive city below.

Patroness of the USA

It appears that every nation in the world has a patron saint. I looked up the various lists of nations, and I found out, in fact, that a good number of countries have more than one patron saint, or, if not a saint per se, they have the Virgin Mary under some particular title as their patron.

The United States of America does not have a patron saint; it has the Blessed Virgin Mary as its patroness: The Virgin Mary under her title of the Immaculate Conception.

Pope Pius IX formally approved a national patroness for our nation. The bishops of the United States gathered in Baltimore at the sixth council of Baltimore decided on May 13, 1846, to petition the Holy Father to give us a patron saint, and they requested it to be the Blessed Virgin under her title of the Immaculate Conception.

On February 7, 1847, the pope formally approved the bishops' request.

What is astonishing about this is that this decision was seven years before the pope proclaimed the formal doctrine of the Immaculate Conception in 1854!

Four years later in 1858, a young peasant French girl had several apparitions of the Blessed Virgin Mary. Her critics told her to ask this woman who she was, the girl asked, and the woman answered: "I am the Immaculate Conception." The young girl was Saint Bernadette Soubirous.

Today, throughout the United States there are hundreds of churches named Immaculate Conception. In 1959, the largest church in the United States opened its beautiful doors in Washington, D.C., the Basilica of the Immaculate Conception, an appropriate name for the capital of the United States whose patroness is that title of Mother Mary!

When we attend Mass for the Feast of the Immaculate Conception on December 8th, I think that we should thank God for the patroness of our beloved country.

Our Lady of Lourdes

I was a student in high school when I first read "The Song of Bernadette." I remember that the book fascinated me. My parish church at home in Chicago had a replica of the grotto in the lower church so I was familiar with Lourdes but not the details.

Later in the priesthood, I was exposed to the book once more. This time I learned a few facts about the author, Mr. Franz Werfel; he was not a Catholic. This fact had no effect on the credibility and authenticity of the work as far as I was concerned; it was still an excellent book; the author certainly did his homework. I wonder how his research and authorship affected his life?

In the Personal Preface, Werfel quoted Saint Thomas Aquinas.

"To one who has faith, no explanation is necessary.
To one without faith, no explanation is possible."

As I have studied the various apparitions of the Blessed Virgin Mary, I have concluded that this quotation is appropriate for all her appearances.

****

On February 11, 1858, Bernadette, her sister Toinette, and their friend Jeanne went looking for wood and came to the Grotto of Massabielle called "the pigs' shelter." It was dirty, damp, and cold. Remember this was the month of February.

The three crossed the icy water; Bernadette suffered from chronic asthma and was not too happy about going across. It is amazing that Bernadette lived as long as she did because she had contracted cholera as a youngster and suffered from extreme asthma. She lived her whole life in poor health including, of course, during her years as a Sister of Charity of Nevers from 1867 to 1879.

Bernadette heard a noise and looked up. There in the hollow of the rock was a small young lady who smiled at her. This was the first apparition of the Virgin Mary.

On February 18, 1858, Our Lady speaks for the first time in the third apparition. Bernadette was ready to write down what the Lady was going to say.

"What I have to say you does not have to be written down."

"Would you do me the kindness of coming here for fifteen days?"

Bernadette was overwhelmed, but who wouldn't be?!

The Virgin said:

"I promise that you will discover here below another world."

Despite her poverty, illness, and lack of education, Bernadette was a deeply happy young person. Here she discovered the Kingdom of God, the Kingdom of Love!

During the seven first apparitions of Our Lady, Bernadette's face showed genuine joy, happiness, but between the eighth and twelfth appearances her face became sad, hard; and she did things that caused on-lookers to question her sanity. For example, she moved on her knees around the grotto, she ate grass, she scraped the ground trying to drink the muddy water, smeared her face with mud and did these things more than once.

Bernadette was performing acts of humility, fulfilling biblical actions,

From a little muddy water came a flowing spring!

"Did the Lady say something to you?" Bernadette responded:

"Penance, penance, penance, pray for sinners."

By penance, as we understand from our own Lenten practices, we mean conversion, a change in our thinking and behavior. We use the word "metanoia."

And we pray for ourselves; we pray for others.

On February 25, 1858, Our Lady told Bernadette to dig in the dirt and drink the water that would appear. She did. On March 1, a woman was cured of paralysis after dipping her hand in the spring. It was the beginning of thousands upon thousands dipping their bodies in that water! I personally can testify to that.

The Blessed Virgin told Bernadette to tell the priests to have a chapel built and have processions held there. I have personally celebrated Mass in one of the smaller chapels and been in the procession. Those were blessings for me!

On the final apparition of Our Lady, March 25, 1858, when Bernadette asked who she was, Our Lady replied: "I am the Immaculate Conception." When Bernadette told that to the priest, Abbe Dominique Peyramale, he knew immediately that the apparition was indeed authentic, that it was truly the Blessed Virgin Mary!

Twenty years before Lourdes, in Paris, in 1830 when the Blessed Virgin gave Saint Catherine Laboure the Medal of the Immaculate Conception the wording of on the medal was clear:

"O Mary, conceived without sin, pray for us who have recourse to thee."

Every time we repeat those word from the medal, we are professing Our Lady's Immaculate Conception.

Our Lady asked Bernadette to bring a lighted candle on each of her visits. It might be beneficial to our spiritual lives to remember that when we light a candle, we are imitating Bernadette and her visits to Lourdes.

Our Blessed Lady appeared to Saint Bernadette Soubirous eighteen times at Lourdes. Others have talked to Mary a few times, but never eighteen. Bernadette had to be overwhelmed by her heavenly Mother's love.

May I share with you something that I think that Saint Bernadette teaches us?

It is something I learned a long time ago in theology: the sacraments that we receive are personal encounters in which the Holy Spirit unites to our God you and me with our particular biography: strengths, weaknesses, the good and bad, etc.

When we walk up to receive Holy Communion, when we kneel in the confessional, when we receive the Sacrament of the Sick, or Viaticum, etc., it is our personal encounter with the Holy Trinity.

Over 7,000 cures have been documented at Lourdes. The Church has investigated and confirmed sixty-nine.

Our Lady of Deliverance

In 1900, the Catholic Church in China was doing well. There were about 800 missionaries from Europe, some 40 bishops, 600 native Chinese priests, and approximately 700,000 Catholics in the country.

During the Boxer Rebellion or, if you prefer, Uprising, things started to rapidly deteriorate. Between 1898-1900 the uprising was tri-pronged: anti-imperialist, anti-foreign, and anti-Christian movement.

The Militia United in Righteousness was known as the Boxers because many of their members had practiced Chinese martial arts or Chinese Boxing.

In June,1900 the Boxers besieged the Beitang Cathedral. Directing the defense during the seize was the French Lazarist, Bishop Pierre-Marie-Alphonse Favier, C.M. of Peking. (A note: in France and a few other nations the Lazarists are known as the Vincentians or Los Padres Paules. Your author is a Vincentian priest).

Bishop Favier, who designed the cathedral, kept a journal during the siege; his descriptions are vivid.

Favier related that the Boxers attacked any Catholic settlement, destroying and murdering: small children were quartered, women burned in church or run through with a sword; men stabbed or shot or crucified. The conduct of the Catholics was exemplary.

The cathedral which housed the Lazarists was besieged by 10,000 Boxers and soldiers from the regular military. Behind the stone walls of the church, were over 3,900 Chinese Catholics and numerous

French and Chinese priests and sisters defended by only forty-one French and Italian marines.

Bishop Favier had stockpiled huge stores of food, weapons, and ammunition, but the large number of refugees necessitated rationing until the siege was lifted by the Japanese military on August 16, 1900.

The Superior of the Sisters of Charity in Beitang, Sister Helen de Jaurias, compared to Saint Louise de Marillac, was among the people behind the walls.

Her diary provides proof of the siege: the need to lodge and feed 1,800 women and children. The rigors of old age and fatigue did her in; she died on August 20.

Bishop Favier summarized the death-poll: 400 were buried, of whom forty were killed by bullets, twenty-five by one explosion, eighty-one by another and one by another. Of the rest, some died of disease but the greater part by starvation. Twenty-one children were buried at one time in one grave. Some were blown to pieces in explosions. Fifty-one children disappeared in this way,

In 1901, Bishop Favier recounted to those at the Vincentian mason-mere in Paris:

> "Every night for two months, the Chinese (Boxers) directed heavy gunfire at the roofs of the cathedral. Why? There was no one there to defend the cathedral. After the liberation, the pagans provided the key to the mystery. 'How is it,' they said, 'that you did not see anything? Every night, a white Lady walked along the roof, and the balustrade was lined with white soldiers with wings. The Boxers, as they themselves affirm, were firing at the apparitions."

Their miraculous survival was attributed to a woman in white, Our Lady of Deliverance. Bishop Favier, Vicar Apostolic of Peking, had a chapel erected in thanksgiving, in the church of Beitang in her honor, Our Lady of Deliverance.

This is an incredible story but substantiated by non-Christians and, at that time, enemies of the Catholic faith.

Our Lady is represented as the Empress of China holding in her arms the Child Jesus, who is depicted as an imperial Chinese prince. The picture of both is stunning by its beauty.

Our Lady of Knock

This apparition of the Blessed Virgin Mary at Knock, Ireland is unique, But, as I have reiterated elsewhere, I have reached the conclusion that every one of Our Lady's apparitions is unique. She forever surprises us, certainly the visionaries.

On the evening of Thursday, August 21, 1879, even though it was raining heavily, a few people saw three figures bathed in light against the rear exterior wall of the parish church, Saint John the Baptist Church.

As they got closer, they recognized Mary, Saint Joseph, and Saint John the Evangelist. Mary kept looking up to heaven with her eyes and hands slightly raised in prayer.

Fifteen people, ranging from six to seventy came and witnessed the vision.

Our Lady was in the center wearing white with a crown on which there was a single golden rose.

Saint Joseph on her right looked toward Mary; Saint John on her left had his hand raised as if was going to give a blessing.

There was a lamb resting on an altar behind them.

The next day parishioners reported the vision to the pastor,

Word spread and pilgrims arrived in Knock by the thousands.

In 1880, a statue of Our Lady of Knock was erected where the vision took place.

In 1971, the Vatican's Sacred Congregation for Divine Worship granted the Knock Shrine the right to conduct anointing of the sick as at Lourdes. Many cures had been reported.

Our Lady came to be with her people, to be present to them, and to share their fate in silence.

The poor Catholics took the apparition as a sign of heavenly approval against wealthy landowners backed by the British government. (The Land War of tenant resistance to evictions that followed the Great Famine.)

What is notable about Mary's apparition in Knock:

+ The apparition happened at a time when Ireland was reeling from the aftereffects of the famine years of the 1840's.
+ This was one of the few times when Our Lady did not appear by herself, when Saints Joseph and John appeared with her.
+ Mary did not say a word, and she gave no mission.
+ Mary taught by her very presence that God cares; God is always with us.
+ It rained heavily but it did not stop the apparition.
+ The young John Curry who was five years old when he witnessed the vision died in 1943 and was buried in New York City.
+ Pope Saint John Paul II paid a visit to the Shrine in 1979 which had been rebuilt in 1975 to accommodate the huge groups of pilgrims.

Our Lady of the Miraculous Medal

Let me say this from the top: this is a misnomer. The medal that Our Lady gave us through the person of Saint Catherine Laboure is really the Medal of the Immaculate Conception as it so proclaims on the front of the medal:

> "O Mary, conceived without sin, pray for us who have recourse to thee."

****

Our Lady started with innocence: a young French girl from a farm in a remote area of France, now a novice in the Daughters of Charity of Saint Vincent de Paul. The young Sister is Zoe Laboure, soon to be named by the Sisters' community as "Sister Catherine Laboure."

On Sunday night, July 18, 1830, at 11 pm, an angelic child (perhaps her Guardian Angel) woke up Catherine and told her that the Blessed Mother was waiting for her in the community chapel downstairs.

Catherine dressed and followed "the child" to the chapel which was ablaze with light as on Christmas Eve.

Catherine knelt at the Communion Rail near the upholstered chair where the priest Director of the Sisters usually sat when he gave conferences to the Sisters.

Before she knew it, Our Lady sat down in the chair, and Catharine knelt at her side, put her hands in Our Lady's lap and listened as Mary talked:

"Our good God wishes to charge you with a mission."

The two conversed. Mary told about the sorrows coming upon France. The whole world will be upset by miseries. Pain crossed Mary's face. There is remedy.

"Come to the foot of the altar.

There graces will be shed upon all, great and little, who ask for them."

Here we hear Our Lady giving words of love and hope.

Our Blessed Mother returned to the miseries coming upon France and the whole world.

"Don't be afraid. The protection of God shall be ever present in a special way. Saint Vincent will protect you. I will be with you myself. Always, I have my eye upon you. I will grant you many graces."

"The danger will be enormous....I will be with you; have confidence....Do not be discouraged. I shall be with you."

It was a refrain of hope. Mary's words promising confidence sounds like the words of a devoted mother to her child! "Have confidence, have confidence."

Mary divulged more about the future problems and sorrows. At first, the conversation was one-sided. Then Catherine spoke from her heart, asking questions which Our Lady graciously answered.

Suddenly, before she knew it, Our Blessed Mary was gone as quickly as she had appeared.

By the time Catherine got to bed, it was 2 am on July 19th. The conversation had lasted a good two hours plus!

****

> I do not know of anyone who touched the body of the risen Mother of God or knelt by her side for three hours and had her hands in Our Lady's lap. This last fact alone is incredible!

> We will see in one other apparition where Mary touches the visionary twice!

****

Saturday, November 27, 1830, the day before the First Sunday of Advent, at 5:30 pm, the community of the Daughters of Charity was assembled for their evening meditation. There was silence; it was time to pray.

Sister Catherine heard the rustling of the silk gown. Our Blessed Lady appeared in the sanctuary standing upon a globe. Only Catherine could see Our Lady.

The Virgin Mary held in her hands a golden ball which she seemed to offer to God because her eyes were directed heavenward.

Suddenly, her hands were resplendent with rings set with precious stones that flashed in brilliant light.

Mary looked directly at Catherine. Mary's lips did not move but Catherine heard her voice:

> "The ball represents the whole world, especially France, and each person in particular.

"These rays symbolize the graces I shed upon those who ask for them. The gems from which rays do not fall are the graces for which souls forget to ask."

Everything happened so fast. The golden globe vanished from Mary's hands, then an oval frame formed around the Blessed Virgin, and written within it in letters of gold Catherine read:

"O Mary, conceived without sin, pray for us who have recourse to thee."

Catherine heard the voice:

"Have a medal struck after this model. All who wear it will receive great graces. They should wear it around the neck. Graces will abound for persons who wear it with confidence."

The tableau revolved, and Catherine saw the reverse side of the medal she was to have struck. It contained a large M surmounted by a bar and a cross. Beneath the M were hearts of Jesus and Mary, the one crowned with thorns, the other pierced with a sword. Twelve stars encircled the whole oval.

Then the vision disappeared.

As Sister Catherine had to depend on others, it was sometime before the medal was struck and distributed to the Sisters and people, especially those who were in need. Because of the remarkable wonders that were taking place in the lives of people, The Medal of the Immaculate Conception became in the minds and hearts of the French "The Miraculous Medal." The nickname has spread worldwide.

The Blessed Mother gave us some practical spirituality:

Come to the foot of the altar
Do not be afraid
Wear the medal around the neck
Have confidence

Our Lady of Hope

There is an active shrine of Blessed Mary in Pontmain, France. The shrine is called Our Lady of Pontain, but it is also known as Our Lady of Hope.

The apparition of the Blessed Virgin Mary occurred at the height of the Franco-Prussian War of 1870. The oncoming Prussian military force was headed for the city of Laval. The village of Pontmain lay between the attacking forces and Laval.

On the evening of January 17, 1871, Eugene Barbedette (age 12) was helping his father in the barn and when he looked out at the sky, he saw an apparition of a beautiful woman smiling at him. She was wearing a blue gown covered with golden stars, and a black veil under a golden crown.

His father, brother, and a neighbor came out to look. Eugene's brother Joseph (age 10) immediately said he too could see the apparition, although the adults could not.

Two little girls came, and they could see the lady. The girls were able to describe in detail exactly what the two brothers had said.

Villagers arrived and began reciting the Rosary. More children described the lady in blue.

As the Rosary continued, the dress' stars began multiplying until it was almost totally gold. The adults only saw three stars forming a triangle.

As they prayed the Rosary, the children saw a banner unfurl beneath the Lady with a message:

"But pray, my children. God will hear you in time.
My Son allows himself to be touched."

Upon hearing the message read aloud, the villagers began singing the hymn "Mother of Hope." As they sang, Our Lady laughed and joined in the singing.

The children were delighted to see the Lady's hands keeping time with the music.

When the crowd changed the hymn to "My Sweet Jesus," the lady's expression changed to sadness and a red crucifix appeared in her hands with the words

"Jesus Christ" about it.

As the people sang "Ave Maria Stella," the cross disappeared, and her smile returned though with a touch of melancholy. Two small white crosses then appeared on her shoulders before Our Lady disappeared behind a cloud. The apparition ended about 9 pm; it had lasted about three hours!

Years later, Joseph Barbedette, now a priest in the Oblates of Mary Immaculate, described the apparition in detail. This time he described Mary's hands.

"Her hands were small and extended toward us as in
the 'Miraculous Medal' fashion."

"Like a true Mother, she seemed happier in looking at
us than we in contemplating."

The same evening of the apparition, the Prussian forces abandoned their drive toward the city of Laval through Pontmain.

The Prussian General von Schmidt related:

"We can't go further. Yonder, in the direction of Brittany, there is an invisible 'Madonna' barring the way."

On January 23, 1871, an armistice was signed.

Our Lady was a pillar of hope for these people in the path of destruction. She is Our Lady of Hope for us during this time of havoc and turmoil.

My Observations:

+ "My Son allows himself to be touched."
+ As they prayed the Rosary, the gold stars began multiplying until her whole dress was almost totally gold. We are talking about gold. This is Mary power.
+ Mary laughed and joined in the singing and kept time in the music.
+ We see changes in her facial expression: from joy to sadness and back.
+ Like a mother, she seemed happier in looking at us,

Two Lesser Known Shrines of Blessed Mary

There are two lesser known shrines among our American faithful. Yet I would like to share them with you: The Shrine of Montenero and The Shrine of Our Lady of Buglose. The first is in Italy, the second in France.

Both Marian shrines are known by many of the Vincentian Family throughout the world.[90]

Our Lady of Grace, Montenero

I have had the occasion to have prayed at this shrine which is very popular in Italy. The Sanctuary of Montenero[91] is the Patron of Tuscany and is situated outside the city of Livorno, Italy.

I intentionally visited the shrine because, at the time, I was giving presentations on Saint Elizbeth Ann and continuing research on her life. Saint Elizabeth Ann Seton had prayed at the shrine in 1803. I was delighted to see that they had a plaque with the recognition of the saint's presence there. A few people in Livorno held the opinion that Elizabeth Ann was converted to Catholicism at this shrine but

---

[90] The Vincentian Family is comprised of those women and men who hold Saint Vincent de Paul as their founder or patron or inspiration. These people may belong to a religious community or lay organization.

[91] Montenero= The Black Mountain

entered the Catholic Church after she returned to New York. I do not know if their theory is accurate or not; only God knows, but it sounds plausible with a caveat or two.

The shrine has an interesting history. According to legend, a shepherd discovered a statue of the Virgin Mary in 1345 and carried it to Montenero which was known as the haunt of bandits. A small chapel was built in honor of this miraculous image; it was expanded over the centuries maintained by Vallumbrosian monks.

The shrine is really in honor of Our Lady of Grace. Mary's role as Mother of Jesus, the source of our grace, gives her the privilege of being the instrument through which that grace comes to us. Saint Bernard puts it clearly:

> "God could have dispensed his graces according to his good pleasure. this means whereby grace would reach you."

Pope Benedict XVI said:

> "Our Lady is like a celestial stream through which the flow of all graces and gifts reaches the soul of all wretched mortals."[92]

During apparitions of Mary, she promises graces for those who pray the Rosary, who attend Mass, and go frequently to confession. As our Mother, she wants us to receive all the graces that we need to obtain eternal life. She is our Mediator who passes graces through her hands, Our Lady of Grace.

While the shrine of Montenero is beautiful, the real attraction for many is in the surrounding rooms and corridors. On the walls hang Italy's largest collection of ex-votos.[93]

---

[92] Benedict XVI, op.omnia, vol. 16, ed. Prati, 1846, p 428
[93] Ex-votos = votive offerings of people giving thanks to Our Lady for saving them in some manner

The collection started in the early 1800s and includes paintings, photos, clothing, reproductions, heirlooms. Many depict near-death incidents and images of avoided fatalities in daily life.

Our Lady of Grace's feast day is February 7.

Our Lady of Buglose

I have prayed a few times at the Shrine of Buglose, France. It is situated close to the burceau[94] of Saint Vincent de Paul. Vincent prayed at the Shrine of Our Lady as a youngster. As Vincent was born in 1581, his time praying had to be around 1600 plus.

Sometime in the 1600's, the Huguenots set fire to the original shrine of Our Lady of Buglose but the statue of the Virgin had been hidden in a marsh. The location of the statue unfortunately was forgotten, as was the memory even that the place had once been the location of a shrine in honor of the Blessed Lady.

Years later, a shepherd found the statue in a marsh where he had led his herd. One of his oxen did not go with the others but had gone into an area of the marsh alone and began to bellow in a strange manner. The shepherd climbed a tree to see what was happening, and saw the oxen licking an object that was half buried in the mud. The shepherd was confused and ran into town to bring others back with him to see what happened.

When the shepherd returned, the statue of the Blessed Virgin holding the baby Jesus in her arms had been revealed. The people removed the statue from the marsh with great care, and the Bishop of Dax took the statue and placed it in his church in Pouy. A procession took place but had only gone a short distance when the oxen stopped and refused to move any further. It was understood that Our Lady desired that her image should stay closer to where it was found.

The bishop accepted the fact. A new church was quickly built,

---

[94] Burceau = birthplace

and the shrine became very popular for a long time. Because of its closeness to the birthplace of Saint Vincent de Paul, the shrine is more renowned for that fact.

Many miracles have been recorded at the shrine, as Buglose is referred to as a land of miracles.

Not only did Saint Vincent de Paul pray at the shrine, but so did Blessed Frederic Ozanam, principal founder of the Society of Saint Vincent de Paul; Ozanam had prayed there months before he died in 1853.

The feast day of Our Lady of Buglose is June 29th.

Our Lady of Fatima

I have had the honor of visiting Fatima twice. The first time was in 1995. I remember the date because that morning upon arriving in Lisbon, I met the Rolling Stones in the hotel lobby and had a pleasant conversation with them. I think that they felt at ease because I did not go crazy about meeting them, and I did not ask for autographs or pictures.

My friend hired a car and driver who drove us up to Fatima where we spent a short time, perhaps two hours.

During the second time at the shrine of Our Lady in 1997, I spent almost six days there at a convention with a large group of the Society of St. Vincent de Paul. I appreciated my free time praying in the adoration chapel and in the church at the tombs of Saints Jacinta and Francisco.

Our Lady appeared to the three children in Fatima for the first time on May 13, 1917.

> "A lady dressed in white shinning brighter than the sun, giving out rays of clear and intense light."

The lady promised to come to the children on the 13th of each month. The children were Lucia (10 years old), Francisco (9), and Jacinta (7).

Mary appeared six times to the children between May 13 and October 13, 1917.

Whenever Mary appears, she usually does so because God has given her a mission to divulge. Amazing, often, these missions are not given to adults to promote but to children.

During the apparitions, Our Lady of Fatima announced the mission: pray the Rosary daily to bring peace to the world and to end the war. She asked them to pray for the conversion of Russia, to do penance, and that God wanted the world to have a devotion to her Immaculate Heart.

Very clear and straightforward.

****

I have had the honor of preaching an eight-day retreat to the novices of the Missionary Sisters of Charity in Nairobi, Kenya. They are dedicated to the Immaculate Heart of Mary. The community was founded to spread the Kingdom to the Immaculate Heart among the poorest of the poor.

Devotion to the Heart of Mary began in the Middle Ages with Saint Bernard of Clairvaux. It was practiced by other saints. Saint Francis de Sales speaks about the perfections of this heart. (The adjective "Immaculate" was not used until later.)

Saint John Eudes in 1643 observed February 8 as the feast of the Heart of Mary.

When sacred scripture talks about "heart," it means our innermost place, the seat of our interior being: feelings, urges, desires, our memory, intellect, and will. The heart is our entire person.

The Immaculate Heart of Mary refers to the interior life of our Blessed Mother: emotions, virtues, her virginal love for God the Father, her maternal love for her Son Jesus, and her compassionate love for all people, including you and me.

What God seeks is our heart, the place where God allows himself to be found.

The Carmelite Sister, Lucia of Fatima, has written about the devotion to the Immaculate Heart of Mary. Sister sees this devotion as essential.

On December 10, 1925, the Feast of Our Lady of Loretto, Mary and Jesus, as a child, appeared to Sister Lucia in her cell in Spain.

The child said:

> "Have compassion on the Heart of your most holy
> Mother, covered with thorns, with which ungrateful
> men pierce it at every moment, and there is no one to
> make an act of reparation to remove them."

Our Lady said:

> "…my daughter…you at least try to console me and
> say that I promise to assist at the hour of death, with
> the graces necessary for salvation, all those who, on the
> first Saturday of five consecutive months, shall confess,
> receive Holy Communion, recite the five decades of
> the Rosary, and keep me company for fifteen minutes
> while meditating on the fifteen mysteries of the Rosary,
> with the intention of making reparation to me."

On December 17, 1927, Lucia was told:

> "He (Jesus) wants to establish in the world devotion
> to my Immaculate Heart. I promise salvation to those
> who embrace it, and these soul will be loved by God,
> like flowers place by me to adorn his throne."

It becomes obvious: Devotion to the Immaculate Heart of Mary
was God's plan, the Son's plan. Our Lady said:

> "Jesus wants to establish in the world devotion to my
> Immaculate Heart.
> I promise salvation to those who embrace it, and these
> souls will be loved by God, like flowers placed by me
> to adorn his throne."

****

I read "The World's First Love: Mary, Mother of God" by
Archbishop Fulton Sheen shortly after it was published in 1952.

The 17th chapter of his book captivated my thought and
imagination: "Mary and the Muslims." I have never forgotten this
chapter.

When in Kenya, I gave a presentation to faculty and students
at a boys' Catholic High School located in a large slum. There were
around 130 Muslim teens in the enrollment. I found it quite easy
to speak about Blessed Mary because the Muslims have a profound
reference for her.

In his book, it was then the opinion of Archbishop Sheen that Our
Lady of Fatima will one day be instrumental in converting Muslims
to Catholicism.

Fatima, Portugal is named after a Muslim girl who converted to
Catholicism when she married a prince in the 13th century. The girl
was named after Mohammed's daughter, Fatima.

Archbishop Sheen believed that Our Lady of Fatima is the most
effective means of converting Muslims to Catholicism. He thought
that missionaries would see that more clearly.

We pray that the Archbishop's opinion might become a reality.

****

I remember seeing the 1952 version of "The Miracle of Our Lady
of Fatima" [95] staring Gilbert Roland, an actor whom I always enjoyed.
I was still in seminary formation at the time.

In August 2020, the newest version "Fatima" [96] was released with
good reviews. I presume some of you have seen the film. I hope so.
Please get a copy to view it with your loved ones.

---

[95] Warner Bros.
[96] Production Companies: Origin Entertainment, Elysia Productions, Rose Pictures;
distributed by Picturehouse.

Our Lady of Czestochowa

Our Lady of Czestochowa or, as she is affectionally called: "The Black Madonna" is the Queen and Protectress of Poland.

The Madonna has a long history; the question: what is fact, what is apocryphal? Whatever, the story is certainly inspiring and possibly truer than fiction!

According to tradition, it is a sacred icon painted by Saint Luke on the top of a table built by Jesus. In our faith, Saint Luke traditionally has been understood as an artist and medical doctor. As Saint Luke painted, he listened to Our Blessed Mother tell of the life of her Son, information he used later when he wrote the gospel. Remember, too. Saint Luke wrote a second volume: "The Acts of the Apostles."

Saint Helena moved the icon from Jerusalem to Constantinople where it was enthroned in a church. It was given to the Princes of Ruthenia as a gift and brought to Poland in 1382 by Saint Ladislaus after an arrow scarred the Madonna's throat during an attack by Tartars.

While Ladislaus was taking the icon to his birthplace, Opala, through Czestochowa, the horses stopped and refused to move. Ladislaus saw this as a sign from God and founded a monastery to protect the icon and placed the image in the Church of the Assumption.

During the invasion of the Hussites, the image was broken into three pieces and struck by a sword making two slashes in the Madonna's cheek. It was repaired.

In 1655, monks begged the icon to deliver them from the invading Swedes and despite being outnumbered, the Polish defeated the Swedes.

King Casimir proclaimed the Mother of God Queen of the Polish Crown.

In 1717, Pope Clement XI recognized the miracles associated with the icon.

In 1920, when the Soviet army arrived at the banks of Vistula River, the people prayed to Our Lady. The following day happened to be the Feast of Our Lady of Sorrows; the Russian army withdraw after the image of Mary appeared in the clouds above the city.

Despite the German capture of Poland during World War II, pilgrims by the thousands secretly travelled to pray at the icon and implore her protection.

The icon is enshrined on Jasna Gora ("Bright Hill"), above the city of Czestochowa in south central Poland.

The miraculous icon is one of the oldest pictures of the Blessed Virgin Mary in the world and one of the reasons I wanted to include an article about her in this book.

Why is she called "The Black Madonna?" Because the discoloration comes from centuries of being hidden and exposed to soot and smoke from candles.

Her feast day is August 26th.

Mary in Belgium

As I have mentioned several times, there are no two apparitions of the Blessed Mother alike; each is unique. Mary's appearances in Belgium are two examples of this uniqueness.

The first apparition of Our Lady took place in Beauraing, Belgium, a town of about 2,000 people.

Mary appeared to five children ranging from 15 to 9, from two different families: from the Voisin family: Fernande (15), Gilberte (13), and Albert (11); from the Degeimbre family: Andree (14) and Gilberte (9).

In the winter of 1932, on the evening of November 29, four of the children walked to a convent school run by the Sisters of Christian Doctrine to meet one of the girls when Albert (11 year old) pointed to a lady dressed in a long white robe. She looked to be between 18-20 years old with deep blue eyes, and a Rosary hung from her arm.

Albert did not hesitate to ask her:

"Are you the Immaculate Virgin?"

The Lady smiled and nodded her head. Albert asked again:

"What do you want?"

Our Blessed Lady answered:

"Always be good."

Over the next weeks, the children saw the Lady 33 times: from November 29, 1932 to January 3, 1933, generally in the garden of the convent-school.

Nobody believed the children, especially Mother Theophile of the school. She forbad the children to enter the school garden where they were seeing the Lady, and they obeyed her. But finally, Sister believed the five.

For the first few apparitions in the garden, Our Lady was already visible when the children arrived. Later, she became visible after they started praying the Rosary.

The Blessed Virgin made three requests:

+ have people pray much
+ have a chapel built
+ have people come here in pilgrimage.

During the December 9th vision, separate medical doctors examined the five children while they were in ecstasy. The doctors pinched, slapped, pricked, shone lights in their eyes during the apparition with no response or ill-effects.

A lighted match was held under one of the girls without any response, and, afterwards without any burn mark; she had no knowledge of the match incident.

On the last appearance, January 3, 1933, according to the children, Mary was more beautiful than they had ever seen her. She identified herself:

"I will convert sinners.
I am the Mother of God, the Queen of Heaven.
Pray always."

Mary asked the girl Fernande Voisin:

"Do you love my Son? Do you love me?

The girl replied: "Yes!"

"Then sacrifice yourself for me."

During the last visions, Our Lady opened her arms, shone more brilliantly than ever, and exposed her Golden Heart. She looked at Fernande and said, "Goodbye."

The apparition is now referred to as "The Virgin of the Golden Heart."

Fernande collapsed in tears; her whole body shaking from uncontrolled sobbing.

After the last vision, many cases of spiritual and temporal favors occurred.

The apparitions were approved by the Bishop of Namur on July 2, 1949. Two cures also were approved as miraculous obtained through Our Lady during the months following.

World War II started a few years after the last apparition and Hitler invaded Belgium. The Shrine of Our Lady of Beauraing became a light of hope for the Belgian people!

Incidentally, the five children grew up, married, and lived great lives with their families.

> Interesting items about this apparition:
> the young age of Our Lady,
> the number of times she appeared to five children, and
> how she engaged different ones during the visions,
> and her identification.

A prayer to the Blessed Virgin:

> "Mother with the Golden Heart, mirror of the
> tenderness of the Father, look with love upon the

men and women of our time and fill them with the
joy of your presence."

****

Almost back to back apparitions, the Blessed Virgin appeared
to one young lady, fifty miles to the northeast in Banneux, Belgium
January 15 to March 2, 1933.

These eight apparitions were to Mariette Beco alone.

The Beco family was not very religious. At 11 years old, the oldest
of seven, Mariette was not intelligent; she did poorly in catechism
class and stopped going to First Communion instructions. Her father
Julian was unemployed and could not care less about Mariette's
religious training. She did have a small statue of Mary and a Rosary
that she had found.

The winter of 1933 in Belgium was extremely bitter. It was dark
at 7 pm. Mariette sat by the front window on Sunday, January 15th. It
was a freezing night. As Mariette opened the curtain, she saw a Lady,
about five feet tall, and exceptionally beautiful. Her gown was white
with a blue sash. She was barefoot with one gold rose in between her
toes. The Lady stood above the ground on a cloud. The Lady did not
seem to be affected by the cold at all.

Mariette thought that she was seeing a reflection from the oil
lamp. She put the lamp in another room. The Lady was still there
when she looked out. Mariette called her mother who saw nothing
but a white shape. "It's a witch." "But she's beautiful. Mama. She's
smiling at me." The mother ignored her.

The girl noticed that Our Lady had a Rosary hanging from her
blue sash. The cross was the same gold as the rose between her toes.

Mariette rummaged through a drawer and found the Rosary
that she had found on the road. She began to pray it. The Lady's lips
moved without saying anything.

After a few decades, the Lady raised her hand, and motioned for

Mariette to come outside. The young girl asked permission to do so, but her mother told her to lock the door.

The Lady disappeared.

No one believed Mariette, and she was afraid to see the priest. A girl told the priest, Father Louis Jamin, but he thought Mariette might have been influenced by the apparitions in Beauraing.

The first vision had a deep effect on Mariette; she returned to catechism class and put herself totally into the material. Father Jamin was impressed with the girl's change and told her to pray to Our Lady for guidance.

On Wednesday, January 18, 1933, at 7 pm, Mariette run in the yard and felt at her knees in a state of silent prayer. Her father, Julien, found his daughter on her knees.

Mariette saw a bright ball fast increasing in size, finally changing into a woman's silhouette. The Virgin was now facing Mariette, no more than three feet away. Mary's feet did not touch the ground. Julien called a neighbor and his twelve-year son, but they saw nothing.

The apparition made a sign to Mariette to follow. Mariette said loudly: "She is calling me!" The girl ran up the road, stopped, and fell to her knees twice near a spring. She heard outside herself:

> "Put your hands in the water! This fountain is reserved
> for Me. Goodnight. Goodbye."

The Lady disappeared; her silhouette became a ball of light fading on the horizon.

Around 10 pm, Father Jamin went to the Beco's home. Julien told the story and made a general confession!

The next day, January 19, 1933, again around 7 pm, Our Lady appeared to Mariette this time surrounded by seventeen people but the girl was the only one who could see Our Lady.

Mariette asked who she was:

"I am the Virgin of the Poor."

They went back to the spring. Mary said:

> "This spring is reserved for all nations, to bring comfort to the sick," whereas the day before, Mary told Mariette that the spring was for her alone.

Just before leaving, she said: "I will pray for you; goodbye."

The fourth apparition was Friday, January 20, 1933. This time, it was around 6:45pm, with thirteen witnesses, including the priest and two journalists, Our Lady made a request:

> "I would like a small chapel."

Our Lady put her hands on Mariette and traced the sign of the cross over her head.

At the end, Mariette lost consciousness.

The fifth apparition took place on Saturday, February 11, 1933, the anniversary of Mary's appearances in Lourdes. At 7 pm, when Mariette reached the fifth decade of the Rosary, Mary appeared in all her beauty. Mariette followed the Lady to the spring, dropped to her knees, dipped the tip of her Rosary into the water.

> "I come to alleviate sufferings," Mary said to her inferiorly.

On Sunday, Mariette made her First Communion from Father Jamin.

The sixth apparition was on Wednesday, February 15, 1933. Mariette had a question from Fr. Jamin for the Lady re her authenticity. The answer:

"Believe in me and I will believe in you. Pray very much. Goodbye."

The seventh apparition took place, Monday, February 20, 1933. At the sorrowful mysteries, Mariette fell into deep ecstasy on her knees with arms in form of a cross heard: "My dear child, pray, pray very much." (The vision lasted seven minutes.)

The eighth apparition, Thursday, March 2, 1933. There were five witnesses present on that night. At the beginning of the Rosary, it stopped raining. The sky cleared and stars shone. Mariette grew quiet and extended her arms.

Our Lady looked more beautiful than ever, but she did not smile. Her face was very serious. She told Mariette:

"I am the Mother of the Savior, the Mother of God. Pray very much."

She put her hands on Mariette's head and blessed her with the sign of the cross.

She said:

"Adieu, till we meet in God."

Mariette understood that this was the Lady's last apparition and she cried.

Observations

+ The apparitions happened in the dark around 7 pm.
+ Mary appeared in the freezing cold
+ After the first apparition, Mariette's father Julien was converted.
+ Mariette had to ran to the spring to catch up with Mary.
+ Mary seemed to progressively become more beautiful in the 8 apparitions.

+ The Blessed Virgin touched Mariette's head twice, very rare in any apparition; I only know of one other apparition: the first apparition to St. Catherine Laboure in 1830.

+ On August 14, 1956, the Apostolic Nuncio to Brussels crowned the statue of the Virgin of the Poor.

Our Lady Health of the Sick

On March 2, 2020, our Vincentian community began our annual retreat. Because of the coronavirus, our lockdown went into effect shortly after.

I do not remember exactly when, but I began praying to Our Lady Health of the Sick daily:

"Our Lady Health of the Sick, stop this pandemic!"

Others too began praying to Our Lady under that title. She was no longer an invocation, a title, from the Litany of Loretto. She was our Mother to whom we implored for freedom from the coronavirus.

From my studies, I believe that Our Lady Health of the Sick primarily means our eternal health, our eternal salvation. The word for health in Latin is "salus" which means not only "health" but "salvation."

Through the centuries, hospitals in Europe and here in the United States have been named "Hotels-Dieu" – "God's Hospitals." I am familiar with Hotel Dieu in New Orleans, and I know of the historic one in Paris. France.

The Blessed Virgin Mary has not ceased to help the sick. The lives of the saints are stories of Mary's power over sickness. A good story from one of the Church's famous saints, Therese the Little Flower:

"When Saint Therese was a little girl, she was given up for dead, but the statue of Our Lady smiled upon her, and she was instantly restored to health, in order to work out her life of extraordinary sanctity" which she manifested as a cloistered Carmelite.

The restoration was not only for the welfare of her soul, but for the greater glory of God.

Saint Ephrem called Mary "The joy of the sick."

Saint Thomas More wrote in a book that he authored when he was in prison:

> "How many men attain health of body but were better for their soul's health that their bodies were sick still."

How true that is. I have been living in a community of brothers and priests, all of whom have physical problems, some more serious than others. I do not want to be uncharitable or unkind, but I have seen men who have died – and elsewhere where I was superior of a house – that verifies that statement of Thomas More.

When I was in Kenya, I got to know about a clinic near us run by the community of Saint Camillus de Lellis. The order than he founded has a scapular of "Our Lady, Help of the Sick." In Rome, a church of their community has a painting of the Blessed Virgin under that title which is attributed to Fra Angelico.

Who can number the Sisters who have administered hospitals and clinics in the United States?

Who can number those nurses, Angels of the Battlefield, who cared for the wounded? What was their motivation? Was not their exemplar the Blessed Mary, the Health of the Sick?

There is an old Irish prayer:

> "O Lady, Physician of the most miserable diseases, behold the many ulcers of my soul."

Saint Elizabeth Ann Seton loved the sick. She told her Sisters:

"Love the sick, they are the blessings of the community."

I recommend that we keep praying to Our Lady Health of the Sick.

Pope Francis composed a prayer to her. He prays:

"O Mary…we entrust ourselves to you, Health of the Sick.

At the foot of the Cross you participated in Jesus' pain with steadfast faith.

….Help us, Mother of Divine Love….

We seek refuge under your protection, O Holy Mother of God… deliver us from every danger, O glorious and blessed Virgin,"

Our Lady of Good Success

I chose this shrine because I presume that most Christians never heard of one of such a nature: "Good Success."

I do not think that many people are familiar with this shrine of Our Lady of Good Success. This is understandable because the shrine is in Quito, Ecuador.

For forty years, between 1594 and 1634, the Blessed Virgin Mary appeared to a cloistered Conceptionist Sister in Quito named Mother Mariana de Jesus Torres. During these years, Our Lady wished to be known under the title Our Lady of Good Success. This apparition is unique for its longevity!

During all this time, Our Lady spoke to Mother Mariana about the crisis that would take place in the Church and society. In fact, Mary conveyed the gravity of this crisis so clearly that it caused the poor Sister to die from the effects of watching what was to happen to the Church in the future.

Mary told Mother Mariana that God was ready to punish the world for three main sins: blasphemy, impurity, and heresy.

Our Lady of Good Success prophesized about the "Total corruption customs" during the end of the 19th and greater part of the 20th centuries due to the reign of Satan in society through Freemasonry.

In this vision, Our Lady foretold that in this time the sacraments would lose their importance and their high esteem. In these times, people would be used as tools of the devil to destroy the Church. Due to the deprivation of the sacramental graces among the faithful, many souls would be lost. There would be a tremendous drop in vocations.

Blessed Mary talked to Mother Mariana about the need for penance, suffering, prayer, and self-denial that would be not only pleasing to God—tools with which her convent would be able to sustain itself but also the Church and the world.

Our Lady of Good Success was clear on what would be the demise of the Catholic Church: a lax and perverse clergy, robbers of dogma, doctrine, tradition, leaving in the darkness without the light of the Sanctuary Lamp (which signifies the presence of Jesus in the tabernacle). Our Lady of Good Success went into detail and gave five reasons for the extinguishing of the light.

The Child Jesus prophesized to Mother Mariana the following:

1. The Dogma of the Immaculate Conception would be proclaimed when the Church will be strongly attacked, and the Pope would find himself a prisoner.
2. The Dogma of the Assumption will be proclaimed.
3. I will preserve the Church, so beloved by me….strongly attacked but never conquered.

Our Lady commanded a statue to be made of Our Lady of Good Success.
Why?

+   So that persons might realize how powerful I am in placating Divine Justice and obtaining mercy and pardon for sinners with a contrite heart. I am the Mother of Mercy and in me there is only goodness and love.

+   When persons seem to be drowning in the bottomless sea, let them gaze at my holy image, and I will be there ready to listen to their cries and soothe their pain.

Our Lady herself requested a certain sculptor to do the statue. I find this to be very unusual in any apparition. When he decided to put the finishing coat of paint on the statue, he went off to buy the paint.

The Blessed Mother promised that she herself would see to its completion. Mother Mariana found the upper choir loft illuminated with heavenly brilliance.

Archangels Michael, Raphael, and Gabriel appeared and bowed before the Holy Trinity as if according to a command. Then they stood before the Queen of Heaven and saluted her. The archangels and Saint Francis took to miraculously finish the statue. It was completed in an instant. The statue became enveloped in light brighter than the sun and became animated as the Queen and Mother sang the "Magnificat." This all took place at 3 a.m., the morning of January 16, 1611.

Bishop Salvador de Ribera of Quito approved Mary of Good Success of the Purification and Candlemas.

It is not possible to enumerate the graces and miracles that have occurred during Mother Mariana's life and after her death through the intercession of Our Lady of Good Success. Many of her prophesies have come and gone – or are some "now" ?!

One observation:

The Blessed Mother appeared to Mother Mariana for forty years. That is incredible. Most people would die just for one appearance of Mary!

Our Lady of Mercy

Our Lady of Ransom was the former name for this feast of September 24th; now we refer to the feast as Our Lady of Mercy. However, Our Lady of Ransom is celebrated in certain places like Vallarpadam (National Shrine of Our Lady of Ransom in Kerala, India) and in the order of the Mercedarians. In England, devotion has been revived but recognized as Our Lady's Dowry."

Human trafficking has been a crime, a sin, for centuries. Today, women, men, children, are being sold into slavery for various hideous reasons: sex, hard labor, house servants, etc. Various organizations do all they can to stop the trafficking.

In August 1218, Saint Peter Nolasco received a vision of the Virgin Mary as she also had asked Saint Raymond of Penafort, and King James of Aragon to establish an order to visit and free Christians in captivity.

Mary was dressed in white with the shield of the order imprinted on her full-length scapular.

Following the Blessed Virgin's request, the Mercedarian Order was constituted in Barcelona, Spain by King James. Pope Gregory IX approved the order in 1235 with Peter of Penafort as the first superior.

The order of the Mercedarians hold that their true founder and patroness is Our Lady of Ransom.

The order had two divisions: those members who prayed and collected donations for the Christian captives and those Knights who actually went to the camps to buy back Christians or, believe it or not, to trade places with them, securing their freedom.

Our Lady of Ransom (of Mercy) is often pictured holding two bags of coins to symbolize the ransom paid.

Our Lady of Mercy wears a crown of twelve stars based on the Book of Revelation.[97]

> "And a great sign appeared in heaven: a woman
> clothed with the sun. and the moon under her feet,
> and on her head a crown on twelve starts."

In honor of the twelve stars of Our Lady's crown, The Little Crown of the Blessed Virgin Mary's chaplet is recited. The chaplet consists of a medal, five Our Father beads and three sets of four beads each with the Hail Mary. It is in honor of Our Lady's Crown of Excellence. The chaplet ends with a Glory be.

Thousands of Christian prisoners were freed by the Mercedarian Order!

(Our Lady of Ransom is patron of Barcelona, Spain.)

****

Piracy for two-hundred years was a nightmare for countries bordering on the Mediterranean.

Capturing Christian ships on the Mediterranean Sea meant confiscating merchandise, capturing manpower for galleys, laborers for farming, soldiers, women for harems, and receiving huge sums of money paid out in ransoms and in taxes on the sale of slaves.

Our Saint Vincent de Paul in 1643 agreed to send men to Barbary to console the Christian captives and prisoners, to instruct them in the faith and in the fear of God. Vincent sent brothers and priests to work from the consulates in Tunis, and Algeria.

---

[97] Revelation 12:1

Captured Christians in Moorish prisons lacked the most basic amenities; food was minimal. They were forced to work on agricultural projects; they did the work of beasts of burden, e.g., they turned the mill wheels.

Reluctant to allow it, Vincent finally agreed for his men to redeem people from slavery. The captives deeply appreciative the charitable service.

From the outset, the Vincentian mission acted as business office for dealings between captives and their families. Letters, gifts, and ransom payments were handled eventually by the Vincentian house in Marseilles and forwarded to Barbary through merchants. It has been estimated that 1200 captives were ransomed at the sum of 1.2 million livres.

Our Lady of Good Help

In the United States of America, we have had twenty-nine reported apparitions since 1944 to 1996, and I do not know how many since have been reported.

I do know personally of someone who does not receive apparitions but who supposedly receives allocutions from the Blessed Mother every month; he has quite a following.

On December 8, 2010, Bishop David L. Ricken of the Diocese of Green Bay, Wisconsin gave formal approval of the 1859 apparitions of the Blessed Mother to Adele Brise. The bishop also approved the Chapel as a Diocesan Shrine, recognizing its long history as a place of prayer and pilgrimage.

The chapel is in Champion, Wisconsin, about sixteen miles north east of Green Bay, in America's dairy land. Over the years, I had gotten to know the area quite well because my oldest sister and family have lived in Appleton, Wisconsin. I often drove around the area and bought cheese for others from the small towns that produced cheeses.

In early October of 1859, Adele Brise, the twenty-eight-year-old Belgian immigrant, saw a woman standing between two trees. The woman was surrounded by a bright light, clothed in dazzling white with a yellow sash around her waist and a crown of stars above her flowing blond locks. Adele was frightened by the vision and prayed until it disappeared. When Adele told her parents what she saw, they said that it might be a poor soul in need of prayers.

On October 9, a Sunday, Adele saw the apparition a second time while she was walking to Mass. She was accompanied by two women, but they did not see anything. Adele asked the priest what to do, and he told her to ask:

"In the name of God, who are you and what do you wish of me?"

Returning from Mass, Adele saw the apparition a third time, and this time she asked the question. And Adele got the answer!

"I am the Queen of Heaven who prays for the conversion of sinners, and I wish you to do the same. You received Holy Communion this morning and that is good. But you must do more. Make a general confession and offer Communion for the conversion of sinners, if they do not convert and do penance, my Son will be obliged to punish them."

Our Lady gave Adele a mission:

"Gather the children in this wild country and teach them what they should know for salvation....Teach them their catechism, how to sign themselves with the sign of the Cross, and how to approach the sacraments....Go and fear nothing. I will help you."

Adele devoted the rest of her life to teaching children. She initially went from house to house, but later opened a small school. Other women joined her in her ministry, and they formed a community of sisters according to the Third Order Franciscans. Adele never took public vows as a nun.

She died July 5, 1896, after fulfilling Our Lady's mission for thirty-seven years!

Our Lady's message, her desire, is simple and straightforward! You notice that she tells Adele "you must do more." Adele was doing good things like attending daily Mass and receiving the sacraments, but she must do more.

Our Lady's message to us today is just as simple. We no longer live in a wild country of 1859, but Mary's messages are still relevant:

Pray for the conversion of sinners
Offer our Holy Communion for that intention
Make a general confession for our own spiritual life
Do more for Mary, do more for her Son.
Teach the children, grandchildren, great-grandchildren the basics of our faith.

And our Blessed Mother tells us:

"Fear nothing. I will help you."

What consolation! What comfort!

A small chapel was built by Adele's father on donated land. Then a larger chapel was constructed. This one bore the inscription in French: "Notre Dame de bon Secours, priez pour nous." The shrine received its present name!

The shrine became a popular place for pilgrimages. A larger chapel was built in 1880.

On the night of October 8, 1871, a firestorm began near Peshtigo, Wisconsin and spread, consuming everything in its path. Nearly 2000 people died in the raging fire. When the firestorm threatened the chapel, Adele refused to leave, organized a procession to beg the Virgin Mary for her protection. The surrounding land was destroyed by the fire but the chapel and its grounds together with all the people who had taken refuge there survived the fire unharmed.

The fire had destroyed about 1.2 million acres, the worst recorded fire disaster in US history. I am not certain that this is the record today after all the forest fires in the Western part of the United States in recent years.

The current building at the shrine was built in 1942. It has an upper Apparition Chapel with a small Apparition Oratory.

The Apparition Oratory contains a collection of crutches left behind in thanksgiving by people who came to pray at the shrine.

Our Lady of the Holy Rosary

On the Feast of the Holy Rosary, October 7, 1958, my class received the deaconate from then the Auxiliary Bishop of St. Louis, Leo C. Byrne. It was a special day for our class as we drew closer to ordination to the priesthood.

Since that day, over the years, the Feast of the Holy Rosary on October 7th, has taken on an added significance for me: one of thanksgiving to God for my vocation to priesthood.

****

On October 7, 1571, there was a naval engagement off the coast of southwestern Greece between two fleets: one of a coalition of Catholic Christian States arranged by Pope Pius V vs a fleet of the Ottoman Empire. The Catholic Christian inflicted a major defeat.

In honor of the victory, Pope Pius V instituted the Feast of Our Lady of Victory, now called Our Lady of the Rosary. October 7th is the anniversary of the battle.[98]

Two years before the naval battle, there was a book published in Venice: "The Spiritual Combat" by Dom Lorenzo Scopoli; it is a spiritual classic still being read today. Saint Francis de Sales carried a copy of it in his pocket for eighteen years.

The subtitle of the book is: "How to Win Your Spiritual Battles and Attain Peace."

---

[98] Pope Clement XI extended the feast to the whole Church in 1716.

You and I face our battles. Probably the greatest two are our struggle against sin and our embracing holiness of life through the love of God and neighbor, the mandate we received from Jesus himself.

It is difficult to win conflicts alone. We need someone to help us: to strengthen us, protect us, and be at our side. That someone is Our Blessed Mother.

Our spiritual weapon is the Rosary. The backbone of that garland of roses is the Hail Mary.

****

In 1208, the Spanish preacher Father Dominic de Guzman traveled to France to defend the faith against the Albigensian heresy. It was another spiritual battle with consequences.

Father Dominic, whom we now know as Saint Dominic, prayed in the community church at Prouille,[99] France. Our Lady appeared to him and taught him the complete Rosary, attaching fifteen promises for those who prayed the Rosary faithfully.

These promises of Our Lady include protection and graces, a decrease in sin, an abundance of mercy, and reception of the sacraments before death.

St. Dominic spread devotion to the Rosary all over the world.

What do we hear the Blessed Virgin telling us in many of her apparitions?

"Pray the Rosary; pray the Rosary; pray the Rosary daily."

What did I recently read?

"One million children praying the Rosary can change the world."

****

On our former seminary grounds, now the Rosary Walk, there has been a mound on the way to Mary's grotto. On the mound is a statue of Our Lady of Victory. My classmates and I stopped at the

---

[99] Prouille is a hamlet in Languedoc. France. It is the cradle of the Dominicans.

mound countless times and said a short prayer; this was seventy years ago. I read that one of the veteran priests said the statue was there before he arrived in 1892.[100] A good estimated guess would mean that Our Lady of Victory has graced our campus for 150 years (or more).

---

[100] Father Jean LaSage, C.M.

Our Lady of Altotting

In German, this Marian shrine is "Unsere liebe Frau von Altotting."

The town of Altotting lies in the heart of Bavaria, about one hour from Munich.

Some of you who have attended the Passion Play in Oberammergau, Bavaria may have visited the Shrine of Our Lady, if not, you were probably close to it!

Interestingly, some pre-Christian tribes in Germany venerated the linden trees besides the oak as sacred. Freya, the goddess of love, was worshipped in linden trees. Public and legal concerns, and even private disputes were decided under linden wood trees in hope that the goddess Freya would provide an aura of charity, truth, and reconciliation. We can see why these trees also were called "trees of justice."

The chapel of Grace which houses the image of Our Lady dates around 660 AD.

Our Lady was carved of linden wood around 1330, a tree to this day venerated in Germany and Austria. The statue has become darkened by the smoke of thousands of candles over the centuries and is popularly known as the "Black Madonna."

Our Lady was already invoked as a Black Mary during the 30 Years War in the first half of the 17th century. This was also when King Maximilian of Bavaria consecrated himself and his country to the Virgin of Altotting by writing her a letter in his own blood as the ink! This letter is kept in the base of the tabernacle under the Black

Madonna. Since then the hearts of the kings of Bavaria have been set to rest in the "chapel of grace."

People apparently valued the mystery of her darkness so much in 1630 that they painted the inside of the chapel in black. As there are no windows, it is dark in there at any time of day.

In 1489, the shrine became a popular pilgrimage site after the miraculous recovery of a young boy who drowned and was revived after his mother laid his body before the image and prayed to Our Lady for a miracle. The Mother of Jesus responded to the desperate, sorrowful mother!

The shrine today is also called the "Lourdes of Germany" due to the great number miraculous healings that have taken place there and because of the million pilgrims who come yearly in search of healing and to ask for Mary's intercession.

At Altotting also, there is the tomb of Saint Konrad of Parzham,[101] a Capuchin brother who died in 1894. He held the position of porter in the monastery for 41 years. He helped whoever knocked on the monastery door, whatever their wish.

Brother Konrad regularly asked the Blessed Virgin to intercede for him and those who asked for his assistance.

The saint served Mass at Our Lady's shrine every morning and spent another hour in prayer before her later in the day; he often presented her with flowers.

His cell and tomb can be visited. In front of it is the "Pope-Linde" which Saint Pope John Paul II planted in 1980. The Pope had come to the shrine with then a young Joseph Ratzinger who was accompanied by his father.

Joseph Ratzinger became Pope Benedict XVI.

In our Marian Meditation Walk – The Ring of Mary – we have a statue of Our Lady of Altotting. It is wonderful to be able to pray to this great Lady whom so many citizens of Germany love so dearly.

---

[101] Brother Konrad was canonized in 1934.

Our Lady Undoer of Knots

Knots.

There is a song:

"Oh, my stomach's tied in knots."[102]

What do we hear people say? "I feel like I'm tied up in knots." "I have a knot in my neck." "Why do I feel like I have a knot in my brain?"

Our lives have knots, some that seem impossible to untie. We have financial problems, marital problems, relational problems, health issues (often serious), fears, things that worry us 24/7, living alone in our big house, unemployment, etc. Knots, big and small.

When we find ourselves facing these challenges that seem to have no solutions, there is someone to go to: Our Lady Undoer of Knots.

We trust in Our Lady, our intercessor. We come to her with faith in God.

We trust in God to answer our prayer—that can change and turn our lives around in full circle if need be.

We turn to Our Lady to untangle our knots.

The devotion to Mary Undoer of Knots began in 1612 with a very unhappy married couple in Germany. The couple, Wolfgang Langenmante and his wife Sophie, were on the brink of divorce.

---

[102] Songwriters Kellin Quinn and James Lawson, BMG: Rights Management

Desperate, Wolfgang sought counsel from a Jesuit priest, Father Jacob Rem.

Wolfgang landed his wedding ribbon to the priest who lifted it up to an image of Our Lady of Snows. And while untying the knots of the ribbon he prayed:

"I raise up the bond of marriage that all knots be loosed and resolved."

The unknotted ribbon became bright white – a sign of The Virgin Mary's intercession. The Langenmantes' marriage survived!

(At the time, a bride and groom were 'tied together' in the wedding ceremony with a ribbon, symbolizing their unbreakable union. In some marriages that I witnessed in Chicago; couples used ribbons with the same symbolism.)

Pope Francis learned about the Marian devotion in 1986 when he was studying for his doctorate in Germany. Pope Francis brought this devotion to Argentina when he was archbishop there. From there, it spread to Brazil, and now it spreading throughout the Catholic faithful.[103]

While visiting the Church of St. Peter am Perlach in Augsburg, then Father Jorge Mario Bergoglio, S.J. of Argentina saw a painting of Our Lady untying the knots in a white ribbon. He became fascinated by the painting and the story behind it. He bought a postcard of the image, and, as a cardinal, he had the image engraved into a chalice and presented it to Pope Benedict XVI.

In the image, an angel hands Mary a white ribbon while another angel smoothed the opposite end. The Holy Spirit appears over Mary's head in form of a dove; her head is surrounded by twelve stars and eight angels.

Mary unties knots in the ribbon while she stands above a crescent moon, crushing a twisted serpent under her heel. (This reminds us of

---

[103] I recommend a painting of Our Lady, Undoer of Knots by Mr. Daniel Mitsui: www.danielmitsui.com

the front side of the Miraculous Medal). Also, those words from the Book of Revelation (which I quoted elsewhere):

> "....a woman clothed with the sun, with the moon under feet and a crown of twelve stars on her head."[104]

What is the knot(s) in your life right now?

Are you willing to let Our Lady help you find solutions to the knots?

Does knowing that Mary is "Undoer of Knots" give you great confidence in her?

> "Mary, Undoer of Knots, by remaining forever Our Mother, you put in order and make clearer the ties that link us to the Lord. Through your grace, your intercession, and your example, deliver us from all evil, Our Lady, and untie the knots that prevent us from being united with God, so that we, free from sin and error, may find God in all things, may have our hearts placed in God, and may serve God always in our brothers and sisters. Amen"

(Pope Francis)

---

[104] Rev. 12:1

Our Lady Seat of Wisdom

I have known the Blessed Virgin under the title of "Sedes Sapientiae" –
The Seat of Wisdom. During my priestly formation, Latin was our
language in liturgy as well as in our textbooks.

In icons and sculptures, Mary is seated on a throne with the
Christ Child seated on her lap. In one 12th century wood carving of
Mary, Seat of Wisdom, she sits on a chair. On her knees, the Child, a
miniature adult rather than an infant, sits with his right hand raised
in blessing and left hand clasped around a book. Both figures are
dressed like royalty and manifest expressions of profound serenity.

This type of Madonna image is based on the Byzantine prototype
of what they call "Container of the Uncontainable." I like this title
of Mary!

The invocation, Mary Seat of Wisdom, is one title in the Litany
of Loreto and originated in the 11th century. Saint Augustine was
the first one to refer to the Seat of Wisdom. Saint Bernard used the
expression three times and applied it to Mary with the words "The
House of Divine Wisdom."

The relationship between Our Lady and Wisdom was further
developed during the Middle Ages.

From the 12th century, a few titles were given to Mary in praise
of her relationship with eternal Wisdom: "Mother of Wisdom,"
"Fountain of Wisdom," "House of Wisdom," "Seat of Wisdom," as
I mention above, became the most common expression; it certainly
has been in my life.

The title "Seat of Wisdom" celebrates the maternal role of Our Lady, her royal dignity (Queen of Heaven and Earth), and her incomparable wisdom and prudence ("the right way of doing"). The French talk about prudence as practical reason, practical knowledge. You notice in every apparition Mary gives practical knowledge to us, for our spiritual life.

Let us join Our Lady Seat of Wisdom in prayer. Let us be so happy to be called a woman or man of prayer!

We celebrate this Marian feast of Mary Seat of Wisdom on June 8th. Throughout the centuries Wisdom texts have been used in Marian Masses, e.g., Proverbs 8:22-31 and Sirach 24:1-4, 8-12, 19-22.

Our Lady of the Cenacle

"Then they returned to Jerusalem...they went to the upper room, where they were staying, Peter and John and James and Andrew, Philip and Thomas, Bartholomew and Matthew, James the son of Alphae'us and Simon the Zealot and Judas the son of James.

> All these with one accord devoted themselves to prayer,
> together with the women and Mary the mother of
> Jesus, and with his brethren."[105]

Mary shows us as Mother of Jesus the example of harmony and prayer at its beginning. She prays with the apostles and disciples in oneness of mind and heart.

She waits there in the upper room, the site of the Last Supper, for the promised Paraclete. She knew the power of this Paraclete, the Holy Spirit; she had experienced his overshadowing while a young teen with the result of her pregnancy with the Son of God.

Mary waits in prayer. She, too, will experience the gifts of the Holy Spirit on the day of Pentecost. The Holy Spirit certainly would not by-pass Our Lady while he touched all the others.

Our Lady of the Cenacle gives us a good example to be people of prayer, liturgical, communal, and personal.

---

[105] Acts 1:12-14

We join Our Lady of the Cenacle as we wait in joyful hope for the coming of Our Lord Jesus Christ.

****

I knew the Cenacle Sisters[106] on Fullerton Avenue while I was pastor in Chicago. The Sisters had a retreat house in walking distance from us. I enjoyed the silence and freedom from the noises of a busy thoroughfare.

---

[106] The Congregation of the Sisters of Our Lady of the Cenacle was founded by Saint Therese Couderc in Lyon, France.

Our Lady Help of Persecuted Christians

On the wall of my room hangs an icon, a Christmas present to me from a priest friend. The icon depicts the Egyptian Coptic Christian Martyrs. Twenty-one construction workers were beheaded on a beach in Sirte, Libya on February 12, 2015 by a militia group with an affiliation with ISIL.

Exactly, there were twenty Egyptians in the group; the twenty-first was a Ghanaian, supposedly originally not a Christian. He could have walked from the beach, but did not, When the terrorists asked him if he rejected Jesus, he reportedly said, "Their God is my God," knowing that he also would be beheaded.

Authorities and authors talk and write about spiritual warfare that rages within us, yet there is a bitter warfare raging outside of us but within our nations. Christians are being persecuted and killed not monthly but daily for the faith. The icon that hangs on my wall constantly reminds me of this.

Our brother Knights of Columbus launches their 18th Marian Prayer Program featuring an icon "Our Lady Help of Persecuted Christians."[107]

The icon depicts Our Lady with the Child Jesus over her heart, spreading her mantle around a gathering of recent Christian martyrs,

---

[107] During the Supreme Convention in Baltimore (2018), the Knights launched this Marian Prayer Program. Mr. Frabrizio Diomedi created the icon.

women and men of various ages, from East and West. In the group are clergy, religious, and laypersons, including one of the six priest-members of the Knights of Columbus who were killed by the Mexican government, one in 1926, four in 1927, and one in 1937.

The four crosses represent an "ecumenism of blood" among martyrs of Roman and Eastern Catholicism, as well as those of Coptic, Armenian, Syriac, and Orthodox traditions.[108]

The icon is striking in its composition and coloration.

We need to pray for Christians who are dying daily for their faith as well as for those who are striving to stay alive for their faith.

---

[108] Saint Pope John Paul II canonized the six in 2000.

Our Lady of Tears

We begin with Sister Amalia Aguirre, one of the first members of the Congregation of the Missionary Sisters of Jesus Crucified. Although living in Campinas, Brazil, Sister had been born and raised in Spain, on the Portugal-Spain border.

Sister Amalia bore the sacred stigmata of Jesus.

On November 8, 1929, a relative's wife was seriously ill; no remedy could save her. In desperation, the husband turned to Sister Amalia as his last hope. He worried about his children; he did not want to lose the love of his life.

Sister called on Jesus in their community chapel. With open arms, she knelt before the tabernacle and prayed:

> "If there is no salvation for the wife of T…then I am ready to offer my life for the mother of this family. What do you want me to do?"

Jesus appeared to Sister Amalia for the first time.

> "If you want to obtain the grace, ask me for the sake of my Mother's Tears."

Sister asked Jesus:

> "How should I pray?"

Jesus taught her the following:

> "O Jesus, hear our prayers for the sake of your holy Mother's Tears!
> O Jesus, look upon the Tears of the One who loved you most on earth and loves you most ardently in heaven!"

Jesus added this incredible statement:

> "My daughter, whatever people will beg me for the sake of the Tears of my Mother, I shall lovingly grant them."

Exactly four months from the above date, Jesus fulfilled his promise.

Sister Amalia was praying in the convent chapel, on March 8, 1930, when suddenly she felt herself being elevated. A Lady of unspeakable beauty approached her. She wore a violet robe, a blue mantle, and a white veil draped over her shoulders which also wrapped her around the chest. With a smile, she approached Sister hovering. She held a Rosary in her hands that she herself called "Corona" (i.e., circle and means Rosary).

The beads glowed like the sun and were as white as snow.

Our Lady handed Sister Amalia the Rosary.

> "This Chaplet is The Chaplet of My Tears that my Son wants to entrust to your Institute as part of his inheritance. My Son has already taught you the invocations. Through these invocations, he wants to honor me in a very special way and, therefore, willingly will grant all graces that are begged for the sake of my Tears."

"The Chaplet will serve for the conversion of sinners, and especially those who are possessed by the devil....
Through this Chaplet the devil will be defeated, and the power of hell will be destroyed. Get ready for this great battle!"

On April 8, 1930, the Virgin Mary appeared to Sister Amalia and revealed the Medal of Our Lady of Tears and of Jesus Bound (tied during his passion).

Our Lady said that all the faithful people who will bring that prodigious medal with love and devotion would receive innumerable graces.

The front of the medal depicts Our Lady of Tears handing the Chaplet of Tears to Sister Amalia (just as it happened a month before) surrounded by the words:

"O Virgin Most Sorrowful, Your Tears have destroyed the infernal empire!"

On the back:

"By Your Divine meekness, O Jesus Bound, save the world from the error which threatens it!"

Jesus has promoted people to be missionaries of the Tears of Mary. He also had made promises to these missionaries. I recommend that you consider membership into being a missionary of the Tears of Mary.

Bibliography

References to other sources can be found in the footnotes on corresponding pages of the text. Here, also, you will find recommendations for further reading for your edification and inspiration.

In Appreciation

I am very grateful Mr. Don Fulford of the Association of the Miraculous Medal, Perryville, Missouri, for granting permission to use photographs of "The Bronze Mary" on the Rosary Walk and any other references to this statue and grounds for the use in this book.

I thank Mrs. Mary Hoehn for the right to photos shot of the author in the Chapel of Mary Mother of God. I am grateful to Mary for all the assistance she gave me for this publication.

CPSIA information can be obtained
at www.ICGtesting.com
Printed in the USA
LVHW042213101121
702879LV00009B/69